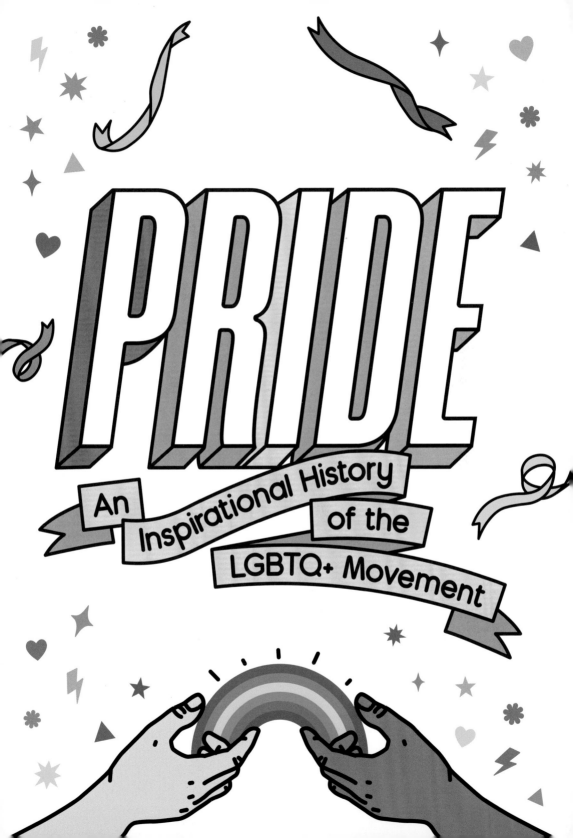

PRIDE

An Inspirational History of the LGBTQ+ Movement

PENGUIN WORKSHOP

An imprint of Penguin Random House LLC, New York

First published in the United Kingdom as *Have Pride: An Inspirational History of the LGBTQ+ Movement* by Welbeck Children's Books, an imprint of Welbeck Children's Limited, part of Welbeck Publishing Group, 2020

First published in the United States of America by Penguin Workshop, an imprint of Penguin Random House LLC, New York, 2022

Consultant Sue Sanders is a prominent LGBTQ+ rights activist, Professor Emeritus of the Harvey Milk Institute, co-chair of Schools OUT UK—an organization that supports LGBTQ+ people in schools—and founder of LGBT History Month and The Classroom.

Visit us online at penguinrandomhouse.com.

Library of Congress Cataloging-in-Publication Data is available.

Manufactured in Canada

ISBN 9780593382943   10 9 8 7 6 5 4 3 2 1 TC

The publisher does not have any control over and does not assume any responsibility for author or third-party websites or their content.

Commissioning Editor: Bryony Davies
Art Editor: Deborah Vickers
Designer: Dani Lurie
Picture Researcher: Paul Langan
Production: Nicola Davey

With thanks to Ayo Babatope, Mohammed Barber, Alex Holdsworth, Ezra Lee Mullin, Mupela Mumba, Shelina, and Dea Urovi.

The publishers would like to thank the following sources for their kind permission to reproduce the pictures in this book.

Key: T=top, B=bottom.

Alamy: /Everett: 62; /Pictorial Press: 16

Getty Images: /Bettmann: 68; /FPG: 33; /Fairfax Media: 80; /Eugene Gordon/New York Historical Society: 79; /Historical: 39; /Pete Hohn/Star Tribune: 95; /Steve Liss/The LIFE Images Collection: 89; /Victor Moriyama: 71B; /Pictorial Press: 23; /Russell: 37; /ullstein bild: 34

Library of Congress Prints and Photographs: 32

Public Domain: 24

Shutterstock: 51, 107T; /AP: 59, 87, 100, 113; /Aflo: 98; /Evan Agostini/Invision/AP: 103; /Piers Allardyce: 88; /Louisa Buller/AP: 91; Colorsport: 101B; /Gianni Dagli Orti: 13; /Salvatore Di Nolfi/EPA-EFE: 104; /Everett: 47, 52; /Jenny Goodall/ANL: 66; /Ink Drop: 9; /Kadena Uk/Mcp: 97B; /Kobal: 77; /Justin Lane/EPA: 99; /Moviestore: 107B; /Georgia O'Callaghan: 101T; /Anna Partington: 114; /Nina Prommer/EPA-EFE: 102T; /Ellis Rua/AP: 116; /Marcio Jose Sanchez/AP: 48; /Morgan Sette/EPA-EFE: 97T; /Snap: 40; /Iain Statham/Sipa: 71T; /Amy Sussman: 102B; /LJ Van Houten: 90

Smithsonian Institution: /National Museum of American History: 92

YellowBelly: 7

Every effort has been made to acknowledge correctly and contact the source and/or copyright holder of each picture; any unintentional errors or omissions will be corrected in future editions of this book.

PRIDE

An Inspirational History of the LGBTQ+ Movement

by Stella Caldwell
illustrated by Season of Victory
foreword by Layton Williams

Penguin Workshop

CONTENTS

FOREWORD BY
LAYTON WILLIAMS

Actor

I was so excited to read this book as I feel it's an important subject for young people. Some may not experience the sort of struggles our community once faced.

Here I was thinking I knew all about LGBTQ+ history . . . clearly not! The book is SO educational, I keep finding myself googling all the amazing people I have read about. It's really fascinating. **If I'd had the opportunity to have all this knowledge at a young age, I would've had a greater appreciation for the queer heroes that paved the way for us.**

It made me think: **What more could I do in my life to make a difference?** I've worked with charities such as Stonewall and Diversity Role Models, leading workshops and talks in schools, and this has got me itching to get back into the classrooms to hopefully inspire more kids.

This is an inspiring read that gives me hope for the future. **We still have a long way to go** until LGBTQ+ people are accepted around the world, but this book highlights just how far we've come.

Take pride in who you truly are, love who you want to love, and respect those who dare to live fabulously free.

INTRODUCTION

SUE SANDERS

Chair of Schools OUT UK and founder of LGBT History Month

You have in your hands a very important book for young people. For too long now the existence and contributions of LGBTQ+ people have been made invisible. This book introduces you to some of the history of our community.

For over forty years I have, in various roles, been trying to make our history accessible to everyone, particularly schools. As chair of Schools OUT UK, I have worked with a dedicated group of volunteers to produce resources for teachers to educate out prejudice and enable LGBTQ+ people in all their diversity to be visible, proud, and safe. It is not an easy task, as you will learn. There have been—and are still—many attempts to discriminate against and silence us.

In 2004 we launched LGBT History Month in an attempt to give schools—and everyone else for that matter—the chance to celebrate and research the achievements of our community. Over the years we have seen a proliferation of events by many different institutions, from libraries to universities and museums, recognizing they have a responsibility to make their collections and work inclusive. For too long LGBTQ+ people have been presumed heterosexual, thus ignoring a really important part of our identities and denying the fact that we have always been here and have played a vital part in so many areas of history.

This book is an introduction. It can't cover everything, so please use it as a jumping-off point to discover more. There are now so many places where you can find information, and the internet offers myriad possibilities. I hope you will enjoy the journey that this book takes you on and begin to discover hidden stories so that you may play your part to make them more visible and usual.

A NOTE:

Over the years, as language has evolved, what our community is called has changed. We have developed the language that is used to be more inclusive: Some of us use "LGBT+," and this book chooses "LGBTQ+," standing for lesbian, gay, bisexual, trans—and the Q can be for questioning or queer. The plus is an attempt to include all identities such as (but not limited to) nonbinary, gender queer, intersex, pansexual, asexual, etc. The use of "queer" is problematic to some people, against whom it was historically used as a term of abuse. It is an action of oppressed groups to reclaim a term of abuse and turn it into an affirmation, though not everyone is comfortable with such an action. It is always wise to ask people how they want to be described and what their pronouns are.

THE RAINBOW FLAG IS A VITAL SYMBOL OF LGBTQ+ PRIDE.

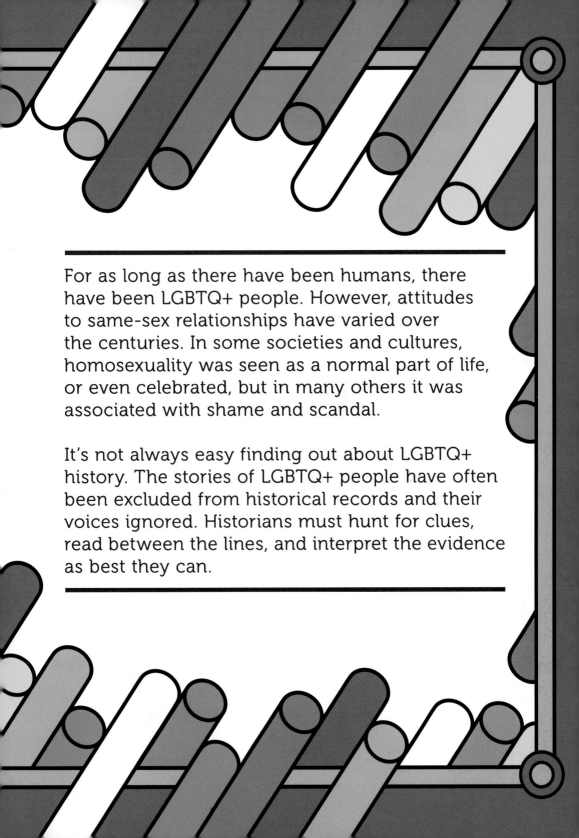

For as long as there have been humans, there have been LGBTQ+ people. However, attitudes to same-sex relationships have varied over the centuries. In some societies and cultures, homosexuality was seen as a normal part of life, or even celebrated, but in many others it was associated with shame and scandal.

It's not always easy finding out about LGBTQ+ history. The stories of LGBTQ+ people have often been excluded from historical records and their voices ignored. Historians must hunt for clues, read between the lines, and interpret the evidence as best they can.

CLUES
FROM THE
PAST

Words such as "homosexual," "bisexual," and "transgender" are relatively recent terms, but that doesn't mean they describe anything new. LGBTQ+ people have existed throughout the ages, playing their part and making their mark in the world.

There is evidence of same-sex love in almost all ancient civilizations. The celebrated Greek conqueror Alexander the Great (356–323 BCE) is widely believed to have been bisexual. The Roman emperor Hadrian (76–138 CE) was so distraught when his male companion, Antinous, drowned that he named an Egyptian city Antinopolis in his memory. Sappho (c. 610–570 BCE), who is considered the greatest female poet of the ancient world, wrote about her attraction to younger women. The word "lesbian" comes from the Greek island of Lesbos where Sappho was born.

LGBTQ+ themes also appear in myths. The ancient Greek god Zeus was so besotted with the Trojan prince Ganymede that he chose him to serve as his cupbearer on Mount Olympus, and he placed him amongst the stars as the constellation Aquarius. In India, ancient Hindu texts tell of gods and goddesses changing their gender and of same-sex encounters. In one Chinese myth, Emperor Ai from the Han Dynasty cut off the sleeve of his robe so he wouldn't disturb his male lover Dong Xian, who had fallen asleep on it. According to Japanese folklore, male same-sex love was introduced into the world by the gods Shinu no Hafuri and Ama no Hafuri.

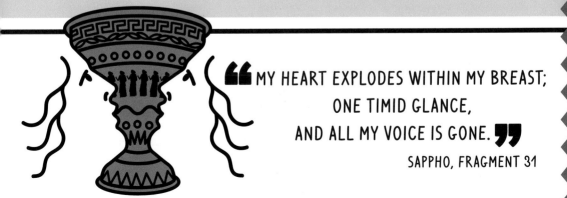

IMAGES OF SAME-SEX AFFECTION WERE
COMMON IN ANCIENT GREEK ART.

OUT OR NOT?

It's likely that people in the distant past didn't think about sexual identity in the same way as we do today. The issue was rarely discussed and certainly not in the language we use now—the first recorded use of the words "homosexual" and "heterosexual" wasn't until 1892, in an English translation of a German book about sexual practices called *Psychopathia Sexualis*. There are very few first-hand accounts of LGBTQ+ lives before the twentieth century, so we must always be very careful about describing the sexual identity of people who never actually "came out" or described themselves in these terms.

"MY HEART EXPLODES WITHIN MY BREAST;
ONE TIMID GLANCE,
AND ALL MY VOICE IS GONE."

SAPPHO, FRAGMENT 31

One of the reasons why historians know that LGBTQ+ people existed in the past is because of the harsh laws and punishments that were put in place to persecute them.

In thirteenth- and fourteenth-century Europe, intolerance of homosexuality rose sharply, and laws were introduced to make it a crime. The reasons for this are complex and involve both political beliefs and religious teachings. In England, the 1533 Buggery Act defined "sodomy" (anal intercourse) as "an unnatural sexual act against the will of God and man." The punishment was death by hanging.

In Britain and the US, sexual acts between women were never specifically targeted by legislation, although that didn't mean lesbianism was considered socially acceptable. Of course, laws didn't stop LGBTQ+ people from feeling the way they did, but the lack of tolerance for same-sex love and a fear of its consequences meant that all too often they either denied their natures or led secret lives tainted by shame and fear.

Some historians believe that iconic figures such as Leonardo da Vinci (1452–1519) or William Shakespeare (1564–1616) were possibly gay or bisexual. Da Vinci was charged with sodomy in 1476, though the charge was dropped. Many of Shakespeare's sonnets, including the famous "Shall I compare thee to a summer's day?" were addressed to a male character known as the "Fair Youth." The subject is hotly debated, and scholars must weigh up the evidence to draw their own conclusions.

> **" I EARNESTLY PRAY TO ALMIGHTY GOD THAT MY UNTIMELY END MAY BE A WARNING TO OTHERS, WHO ARE WALKING ON THE SAME PATH. OH! MAY MY SHAMEFUL DEATH PUT A STOP TO THAT DREADFUL CRIME! "**
>
> THE DYING WORDS AND CONFESSION OF DAVID THOMAS MYERS, WHO WAS HANGED IN ENGLAND IN 1812 FOR AN "ABOMINABLE CRIME" WITH THOMAS CROW

> **SHALL I COMPARE THEE TO A SUMMER'S DAY?
> THOU ART MORE LOVELY AND MORE TEMPERATE.
> ROUGH WINDS DO SHAKE THE DARLING BUDS OF MAY,
> AND SUMMER'S LEASE HATH ALL TOO SHORT A DATE.**
>
> WILLIAM SHAKESPEARE, SONNET 18

TWO-SPIRIT PEOPLE

Native American culture has a long history of "two-spirit people." Some tribal members were believed to possess the spirits of both male and female genders. It was thought that they had spiritual gifts beyond ordinary people, so they were often respected as leaders or teachers. However, European colonial settlers arriving in the fifteenth and sixteenth centuries were horrified to find native people practicing same-sex relationships, and they were determined to stamp out this "vice" with force. By the 1800s, the tradition had been largely suppressed.

ANNE LISTER

1791–1840

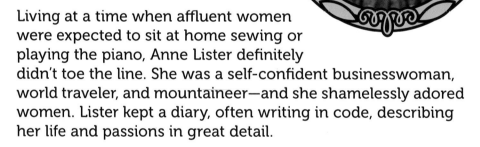

Living at a time when affluent women were expected to sit at home sewing or playing the piano, Anne Lister definitely didn't toe the line. She was a self-confident businesswoman, world traveler, and mountaineer—and she shamelessly adored women. Lister kept a diary, often writing in code, describing her life and passions in great detail.

Lister was born in the Yorkshire town of Halifax, England. Her mother found it hard to cope with her daughter's tomboyish behavior and sent her to boarding school. There, Lister fell passionately in love with another pupil, Eliza, with whom she shared an attic bedroom. Writing in what she thought was an unbreakable code made up of Greek and algebra symbols, she recorded her intense feelings in her diary. Lister later rejected Eliza, who was heartbroken and was eventually committed to a lunatic asylum.

In 1826, Lister inherited her uncle's estate at Shibden Hall. Dressing in unfashionable black clothes, she described herself as a "gentleman," and the locals came to know her as "Gentleman Jack." Lister became a competent businesswoman, but also an efficient seductress, recording her many conquests in great detail.

In time, Lister became besotted with a young woman called Mariana. When Mariana announced she was going to marry a wealthy widower, Lister was distraught. She gave vent to her rage in her diary: "She believed herself . . . over head and ears in love. Yet she sold her person to another."

> **"I LOVE, & ONLY LOVE, THE FAIRER SEX & THUS BELOVED BY THEM IN TURN, MY HEART REVOLTS FROM ANY OTHER LOVE THAN THEIRS. "**
>
> ANNE LISTER, 1821

After a string of flirtations, Lister turned her attention to an heiress called Ann Walker. Lister's feelings lacked the intensity of her passion for Mariana, but Ann had a fortune and would make an ideal "wife." Lister wanted to live with Ann at Shibden Hall like a married couple. When her proposal was accepted, Lister wrote in her diary, "I believe I shall succeed with her. If I do, I will try to make her happy."

The women's union created a scandal, but Lister was too thick-skinned to care what society thought. In 1838, the pair traveled to the Pyrenees Mountains in France, where Lister became the first person to officially climb Vignemale. The following year, they set off on a long tour of Europe. At the Black Sea in Russia, Lister developed a fever and died at the age of 49.

In the 1890s, Lister's relative John Lister came across the diaries and partially decoded them—he was shocked at what he read. He hid them behind a wall panel—some historians believe he was gay and didn't want to draw attention to himself. Rediscovered in the 1930s, they were fully deciphered in 1988 and published as *I Know My Own Heart*.

Today Lister is an important figure and the subject of books and TV programs. Her diaries reveal that she wasn't always a nice person. She could be controlling and selfish—but she was also completely at ease with her sexual identity. Lister knew she was different from what society expected of her, but she was unashamed of that difference. In an age when the word "lesbian" was not in use, Lister certainly had pride.

ANNE'S HOME, SHIBDEN HALL

PERSECUTION BEFORE 1900

342 CE

As Christianity flourishes in Europe, attitudes toward same-sex relationships begin to harden. The late Roman Empire passes a law outlawing same-sex marriage.

529 CE

The Byzantine emperor Justinian outlaws homosexuality (the Justinian Code). Homosexual acts are linked to adultery and as such are seen as sinful.

1102

The Catholic Council of London condemns homosexuality as a sin.

Homosexuality is criminalized in Russia, though it is rarely enforced.

16TH AND 17TH CENTURIES

1610

1625

1832

The Spanish Inquisition is established to root out religious heresy and immoral behavior by brutal means. Between 1570 and 1630, it holds hundreds of trials for sodomy, and many people are executed.

Virginia is the first US colony to make sodomy a crime, with the death penalty for offenders.

Richard Cornish is hanged in Virginia. It is the first documented execution for sodomy in the American colonies.

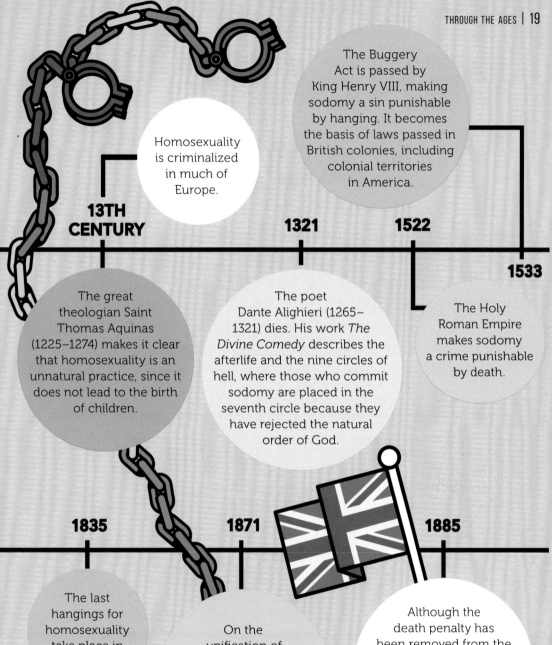

Homosexuality is criminalized in much of Europe.

13TH CENTURY

The Buggery Act is passed by King Henry VIII, making sodomy a sin punishable by hanging. It becomes the basis of laws passed in British colonies, including colonial territories in America.

1321

1522

1533

The great theologian Saint Thomas Aquinas (1225–1274) makes it clear that homosexuality is an unnatural practice, since it does not lead to the birth of children.

The poet Dante Alighieri (1265–1321) dies. His work *The Divine Comedy* describes the afterlife and the nine circles of hell, where those who commit sodomy are placed in the seventh circle because they have rejected the natural order of God.

The Holy Roman Empire makes sodomy a crime punishable by death.

1835

1871

1885

The last hangings for homosexuality take place in Britain.

On the unification of Germany, "Paragraph 175" in the criminal code makes homosexuality between men a crime.

Although the death penalty has been removed from the British penal code, the Criminal Law Amendment Act makes any homosexual activity between men a punishable crime.

BENEATH THE RADAR

The eighteenth and nineteenth centuries were a time of great risk for LGBTQ+ people, but also of increased opportunity. As people moved from rural communities to the expanding cities, there were more chances for LGBTQ+ people to meet each other, though social disapproval and the fear of punishment forced them "underground."

In 1791, during the French Revolution, France removed homosexuality from its penal code, meaning it was no longer illegal between consenting adults. The Napoleonic Code of 1804 extended the law to those countries occupied by France, including the Netherlands and some western German regions—though in Germany, homosexuality was later recriminalized. This was an early step for gay rights, though discrimination remained.

In nineteenth-century America, some free thinkers began to shake things up. Ralph Waldo Emerson (1803–1882) and Henry David Thoreau (1817–1862) were philosophers and writers who stressed the importance of individual freedom and railed against conformity. Both wrote about same-sex desire, though there is no evidence that either man was gay.

Walt Whitman, one of America's best-loved poets, is widely believed to have been gay or bisexual. He never actually "came out" or had an openly gay relationship, but his poetry contains passages that clearly celebrate male love. For this reason, some argue that Whitman is one of the earliest voices of the gay liberation movement.

> **"** FOR THE ONE I LOVE MOST LAY SLEEPING BY ME
> UNDER THE SAME COVER IN THE COOL NIGHT,
> IN THE STILLNESS IN THE AUTUMN MOONBEAMS HIS
> FACE WAS INCLINED TOWARD ME,
> AND HIS ARM LAY LIGHTLY AROUND MY BREAST—
> AND THAT NIGHT I WAS HAPPY. **"**

WALT WHITMAN
"WHEN I HEARD AT THE CLOSE OF THE DAY," *LEAVES OF GRASS*

Another much-loved poet of nineteenth-century America is Emily Dickinson. The ambiguous style and imagery of her striking poetry has led to speculation that she was a lesbian, a theory given weight by the passionate letters she wrote to her sister-in-law, Susan Gilbert. One such letter reads, "Now, farewell, Susie . . . I add a kiss, shyly, lest there is somebody there! Don't let them see, will you Susie?" People have long been fascinated with the idea of Dickinson as an old-fashioned spinster who shut herself away from society, but it's quite possible that, like so many others of her time, she was forced to suppress who she really was.

MOLLY HOUSES

In eighteenth- and nineteenth-century London, a "molly" or "moll" was a slang term for a gay man, and "molly houses" were pubs or coffee houses where they could meet and socialize. However, these places were the scenes of many arrests. Legal records show that in the eighteenth century, around thirty molly houses were investigated. In the 1720s, a spate of raids led to many men being hanged.

In 1861, the death penalty for homosexuality was removed from the British penal code. However, the Criminal Law Amendment of 1885 made any kind of homosexual act between men a crime under the term "gross indecency." The vagueness around the law meant that men were easily blackmailed, and it soon became known as the "Blackmailer's Charter." Oscar Wilde famously fell victim to it ten years later.

In response to this kind of persecution, the nineteenth century saw the birth of the first gay activism. Karl Heinrich Ulrichs (1825–1895) was a German writer who is seen as a gay-rights pioneer. In 1854, he resigned from his job as a lawyer after his homosexuality was discovered. Ulrichs called himself an "Urning," believing he had "a female soul trapped inside a male body." He argued that this was something that people were born with, and therefore couldn't be wicked.

In 1867, Ulrichs bravely stood up at the Congress of German Jurists in Munich to call for a repeal of all anti-homosexual laws. A few years later he wrote, "The Urning, too, is a person. He, too, therefore has inalienable rights. . . . Legislators have no right to veto nature."

> **UNTIL MY DYING DAY I WILL LOOK BACK WITH PRIDE WHEN . . . I FOUND THE COURAGE TO COME FACE TO FACE IN BATTLE AGAINST THE SPECTRE OF AN AGE-OLD, WRATHFUL HYDRA, WHICH FOR TIME IMMEMORIAL HAS BEEN INJECTING POISON INTO ME AND INTO MEN OF MY NATURE.**
>
> KARL HEINRICH ULRICHS, *RAGING SWORD*, 1868

MAGNUS HIRSCHFELD BECAME A TARGET FOR RIGHT-WING ATTACKS.

THE SCIENTIFIC-HUMANITARIAN COMMITTEE

The Scientific-Humanitarian Committee, founded in Germany in 1897, is thought to be the world's earliest LGBTQ+ rights organization. It was set up by Magnus Hirschfeld (1868–1935), a Jewish doctor who realized that many of his LGBTQ+ patients had poor mental health because of the way they were treated by society. Arguing that sexuality was something people were born with and not a choice, he fought for social acceptance and to overturn Germany's antigay laws. The Committee's motto was *per scientiam ad justitiam*, which means "through science to justice."

HAVE YOU HEARD OF?

Chevalier d'Éon (1728–1810)
This colorful French character traveled to England as a male spy and returned as a female writer and celebrity.

Jane Addams (1860–1935)
A great American social reformer and activist who lived with her partner, Mary Rozet Smith, for forty years.

George Cecil Ives (1867–1950)
An English poet who founded a secret society for gay men in 1897 called the Order of Chaeronea.

OSCAR WILDE

1854–1900

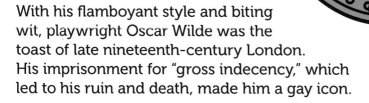

With his flamboyant style and biting wit, playwright Oscar Wilde was the toast of late nineteenth-century London. His imprisonment for "gross indecency," which led to his ruin and death, made him a gay icon.

Born in Dublin in Ireland, Wilde studied at Trinity College Dublin, and then Oxford University. He became involved in the aesthetic movement, which promoted the idea of art existing solely for beauty. Wilde dressed extravagantly and adopted exaggerated mannerisms, and, after moving to London, was determined to find celebrity. He socialized at fashionable venues, published a book of poetry in 1881, and then traveled around North America on a lecture tour, meeting writers such as Walt Whitman.

In 1884, Wilde married Constance Lloyd, and they had two sons whom he adored. With a family to support, he became a magazine editor and published a collection of children's stories, *The Happy Prince and Other Tales* (1888). In 1891, Wilde published his only novel, *The Picture of Dorian Gray*. Victorian society was shocked by the book's coded references to homosexuality and its apparent celebration of decadence. He also found critical acclaim as a playwright, penning hugely popular plays such as *The Importance of Being Earnest* (1895).

Meanwhile, in 1891, Wilde had met Lord Alfred Douglas, or "Bosie," and the two began a tempestuous affair. In one letter to Bosie, Wilde wrote, "I can't live without you." When Bosie's father, the powerful Marquis of Queensbury,

accused Wilde of homosexuality, Wilde unwisely sued him for libel. Queensbury was acquitted, and Wilde was charged with gross indecency. He was tried, convicted, and sentenced to two years' hard labor.

In various prisons, Wilde was kept in total isolation and forced to work a treadmill for many hours a day—a grueling physical task that had no purpose except punishment. While in Reading Gaol, he composed one of the greatest love letters ever written, *De Profundis* ("From the Depths"). Framed as a letter to Bosie, it contains his thoughts on their relationship and his spiritual journey. It was only published after Wilde's death.

On his release from prison, Wilde was bankrupt and in poor health. He moved to Europe, where he was briefly reunited with Bosie and occasionally joined by friends. He never saw his beloved sons again. Suffering frequent public abuse, he wrote, "My existence is a scandal." Wilde died from meningitis in a run-down Paris boarding house, aged forty-six.

In 2017, Wilde was pardoned by the British government for his conviction under "Turing's Law," which acquitted men who had been convicted in the past because of their sexuality. His voice, as that of a man who fell from grace and ultimately died for his refusal to conform, makes Wilde an important symbol of the LGBTQ+ community's fight against ignorance and hatred.

> **TO REGRET ONE'S OWN EXPERIENCES IS TO ARREST ONE'S OWN DEVELOPMENT. TO DENY ONE'S OWN EXPERIENCES IS TO PUT A LIE INTO THE LIPS OF ONE'S OWN LIFE. IT IS NO LESS THAN A DENIAL OF THE SOUL.**
>
> OSCAR WILDE, EXTRACT FROM *DE PROFUNDIS*, WRITTEN IN READING GAOL

WHY I HAVE PRIDE

Name
DEA UROVI

Age
19

Identifies as
NONBINARY

When I was young, I was taught that the world only has two genders.

I first felt the pressure to fit in when I was five. I would wear my favorite soccer team's shirts and play with the boys. At times I thought I was one of them, too. As I discovered the difference between skirts and shorts, buzz cuts and ponytails, nail polish and trainers, it took me some time to accept the fact that nothing is really gendered—we put categories in place because we are scared.

Only recently, I realized that there is no one way of "looking" like a boy, a girl, or something in between. Becoming the person I have always wanted to be has not been an easy ride: I have had the privilege to have very accepting friends and family, but morphing into myself has meant that I have had to lose some people on the way. In those moments of grief, I tried to surround myself with people from my community as this has helped me become happier in my own skin.

I think if I could go back and give some advice to my younger self I would tell them that they have all the time in the world to explore their gender and sexuality. When I was younger, I put a lot of pressure on myself because I felt like I had to prove something to my friends and family. Now I know that there is nothing wrong with taking some time to find out who you are and your place in this world, and I think that welcoming and embracing change is really helpful, too.

> # I HAVE PRIDE BECAUSE MY EXISTENCE AT TIMES FEELS LIKE AN ACT OF PROTEST.

I have pride because, even at the cost of everything and everyone else, I have decided to be myself. However, I would like you to realize you can be proud and still find it hard to accept yourself. You can be scared to be who you want to be and still hold faith in who you are.

I don't fit into people's ideas of who I should be, what I should wear, and how I should act. But your sexuality and gender identity are still valid, no matter how young or at what stage of your journey you are.

You exist, you are here, and you are valid.

THE
SEEDS
OF
CHANGE

As the twentieth century dawned, some extraordinary people were brave enough to raise their heads above the parapet and speak up for what they knew was right. In Germany, Magnus Hirschfeld and his Scientific-Humanitarian Committee tirelessly campaigned for LGBTQ+ rights, while in the US, Henry Gerber set up the country's first gay-rights organization.

The 1920s saw some relaxation of antigay attitudes in cities like Berlin and New York, but that trend was violently reversed in the 1930s as the Great Depression spread economic fear and Adolf Hitler rose to power in Germany.

THE BIRTH OF LGBTQ+ RIGHTS

Oscar Wilde's sensational trials at the close of the nineteenth century were widely discussed in the European and American press, bringing the issue of homosexuality out into the open. Horrified by what she described as the "great injustice" of Wilde's treatment was political activist Emma Goldman (1869–1940). A Russian emigrant living in New York City, she spoke publicly in favor of LGBTQ+ rights.

As we have already seen, Magnus Hirschfeld was making determined efforts in Germany to educate the public on LGBTQ+ issues, which had resulted in the relaxing of antigay laws following the First World War (1914–1918). In 1919, he opened the Institute for Sexual Research, and the World League for Sexual Reform was founded in 1928. Hirschfeld toured Europe, speaking to huge crowds, and later he went to the US and Asia.

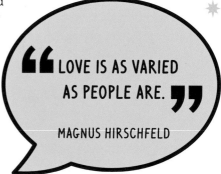

" LOVE IS AS VARIED AS PEOPLE ARE. "

MAGNUS HIRSCHFELD

Someone who was greatly influenced by German reforms was Henry Gerber (1892–1972). A soldier who had served in the US army in Berlin after the First World War, Gerber hoped for the same progress in the US. In 1924, he founded America's first gay-rights organization, called the Society for Human Rights. The Society issued a publication called *Friendship and Freedom*, but it only lasted two issues. In 1925, police raided Gerber's home, and he was jailed. The charges were eventually dropped, but Gerber lost his post office job for "conduct unbecoming a postal worker."

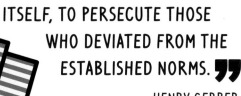

❝ I HATED THIS [AMERICAN] SOCIETY WHICH ALLOWED THE MAJORITY, FREQUENTLY CORRUPT ITSELF, TO PERSECUTE THOSE WHO DEVIATED FROM THE ESTABLISHED NORMS. ❞

HENRY GERBER
ONE MAGAZINE, 1962

SECRET CODES

Being LGBTQ+ in the past could be dangerous, so people developed clever ways to communicate. Oscar Wilde often wore a green carnation on his lapel, which could have been a hint about being gay. In the early twentieth century, red accessories like cravats were used to say *I'm gay*. From 1900, British gay men often spoke a secret language called Polari, based on slang words. For example, men and women were *omees* and *palones*, while a gay man was . . . an *omee-palone*!

In France, homosexuality had been decriminalized in 1791. This allowed LGBTQ+ culture to flourish, but mostly still underground. In the early twentieth century, Paris became known as the bohemian capital of Europe, attracting writers and artists from around the world —many of them LGBTQ+. One such writer was the American playwright and poet Natalie Clifford Barney (1876–1972). She published her first book of poems in 1900,

> **"PARIS HAS ALWAYS SEEMED TO ME THE ONLY CITY WHERE YOU CAN LIVE AND EXPRESS YOURSELF AS YOU PLEASE."**
> NATALIE CLIFFORD BARNEY

Some Portrait Sonnets of Women, with openly lesbian themes. Barney's "salons"— gatherings where artists could discuss their work—drew famous writers like T. S. Eliot, James Joyce, and Colette. Firmly opposed to monogamy, Barney had a string of lesbian relationships, including with Dolly Wilde, the niece of Oscar Wilde.

In the US, Prohibition (the banning of alcohol) came into force in 1920. However, the result was the opposite of what the authorities had intended—it got the party started! All sorts of people were thrown together as they sought out places where they could get a drink. Illegal bars, called "speakeasies," thrived, and so did gay culture, especially in New York. Masquerade balls, or "drag balls," had begun in the late nineteenth century, but in the 1920s they became part of a highly visible LGBTQ+ scene.

A backlash was on its way though, and the brief freedoms of the "Roaring Twenties" would soon fall away. It would be a long time before LGBTQ+ culture would be allowed to raise its head so publicly again.

NATALIE CLIFFORD BARNEY'S NICKNAME WAS "THE AMAZON."

AT "LE MONACLE," A CLUB FOR WOMEN IN 1920s PARIS, PATRONS OFTEN DRESSED AS MEN.

GERTRUDE STEIN (1874–1946)

American-born Gertrude Stein moved to Paris in 1902, where she became a collector of art. Her apartment became a hot spot for artists and writers, and she regularly hosted talents like writer Ernest Hemingway and artist Pablo Picasso. In 1907, Stein met the woman she would share the rest of her life with—Alice B. Toklas—and the pair made no secret of their relationship. Stein's memoir, *The Autobiography of Alice B. Toklas* (1933), became a best seller, and Stein shot to fame—both for her writing and her boundary-breaking lifestyle.

LILI ELBE

1882–1931

Assigned male at birth, Danish painter Lili Elbe struggled throughout her life with the feeling that she was trapped in the wrong body. In 1930, she became one of the very first documented people to undergo gender-reassignment surgery.

While studying art in Denmark's capital, Copenhagen, Lili fell in love with artist Gerda Gottlieb. The pair married in 1904, and Lili began working as a landscape painter, while Gerda created art-deco portraits of fashionable women. On one occasion, an actress failed to show up to model for Gerda, and a friend playfully suggested that the slight-framed Lili could pose instead. Reluctant at first, Lili agreed to pose and later wrote in a journal, "I cannot deny that I enjoyed myself in this disguise. I liked the soft feel of women's clothing and felt very much at home in it from the first moment."

Becoming a regular model for Gerda's work, Lili had a moment of startling realization: The woman in the portraits was the woman Lili understood herself to be.

In 1912, gossip began to spread that Gerda's model was in fact Lili. As the scandal engulfed the couple, they decided to move to Paris, where Lili hoped to live openly as a woman. However, despite living in a more accepting environment, Lili felt less and less able to live what seemed to be a half-life. In desperation, doctors were consulted, and Lili was wrongly diagnosed with the serious mental disorder schizophrenia.

> **" I AM FINISHED. LILI HAS KNOWN THIS FOR A LONG TIME. THAT'S HOW MATTERS STAND. AND CONSEQUENTLY SHE REBELS MORE VIGOROUSLY EVERY DAY. "**
>
> LILI WEGENER'S JOURNAL

In the late 1920s, Lili heard about the pioneering research of German doctor Magnus Hirschfeld. His radical ideas included the concept of "sexual intermediaries," which had sixty-four categories and included transgender people like Lili, who felt they belonged to the opposite sex.

Hirschfeld proposed major surgery to change Lili's body from male to female. This was revolutionary at the time, and the surgery was highly experimental. After three surgeries, Lili was legally able to adopt the name Lili Elbe. Lili chose her surname for the Elbe River that flows through Dresden in Germany, where she was treated. In 1931, Lili had one final surgery, but sadly she developed an infection from which she never recovered.

A true transgender pioneer, Lili lived at a time when gender variance was barely understood. However, her desire to live as a woman was so strong that she realized risking surgery was the only way in which she could feel "complete." Lili saw her death was near, but as she wrote to her sister, "That I, Lili, am vital and have a right to life I have proved by living for 14 months. It may be said that 14 months is not much, but they seem to me like a whole and happy human life."

THE
BACKLASH

The crash of the US stock market in 1929 triggered the Great Depression and in turn led to a crackdown on "immoral" behavior. During this period, many people were out of work, and there was a belief that perhaps the liberal values of the Roaring Twenties had allowed this financial catastrophe to happen.

In the US, Prohibition ended in 1933 and, along with it, the speakeasies that had helped gay culture to thrive. Female impersonators were barred from "pansy clubs," and in London, too, there was a clampdown. In one private drag ball organized by "Lady Austin" in 1933, sixty men were arrested in a police raid, and twenty-seven of them were given jail sentences.

The Hays Code was a list of rules introduced to the US film industry in 1930 to shape—and stifle—filmmaking. Films were to be "moral" and to encourage "correct thinking." As a result, nudity, swearing, and homosexuality were all banned. LGBTQ+ stars were forced to keep their sexuality under wraps. Some were even pressured to enter "lavender marriages" to give audiences the appearance of a "wholesome" home life.

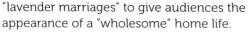

Rumors swirled around Hollywood for years that stars such as Cary Grant, Katharine Hepburn, and Randolph Scott all had same-sex relationships—it's said that Tallulah Bankhead and Billie Holliday dated—but given the atmosphere of secrecy at the time, we will never know for sure.

THE WELL OF LONELINESS

In 1928, the lesbian novel *The Well of Loneliness*, by Radclyffe Hall (1880–1943), was published. Hall, a lesbian, wrote to her publisher, "I have put my pen at the service of some of the most persecuted and misunderstood people in the world." Although many admired Hall's bravery, there was a backlash. "I'd rather give a healthy boy or a healthy girl a vial of prussic acid [hydrogen cyanide] than this novel," declared the editor of the *Sunday Express*. Following a trial, the book was ruled "obscene" and banned in Britain, though it was published in the US after a lengthy court battle. It was not until 1949, after Hall's death, that it was released in Britain.

" OUR LOVE MAY BE FAITHFUL EVEN UNTO DEATH AND BEYOND—YET THE WORLD WILL CALL IT UNCLEAN. "

RADCLYFFE HALL
THE WELL OF LONELINESS

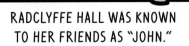

RADCLYFFE HALL WAS KNOWN TO HER FRIENDS AS "JOHN."

Like New York, Berlin had a thriving LGBTQ+ culture in the 1920s. There were many gay-and-lesbian bars and cafés, and open displays of gay nightlife. Of course, these developments didn't mean that the discrimination and persecution of the LGBTQ+ community had disappeared, but they did seem to signal that things might be changing.

However, as the Depression spread economic anxiety, Europe's fascist parties preached against a tolerance of "undesirable people" and minorities. The leader of Germany's Nazi Party, Adolf Hitler, saw homosexuality as a threat to his ideal of a pure race, especially since male partnerships could not bear children. In May 1933, he banned gay organizations. The Institute for Sexual Research, opened by Magnus Hirschfeld in 1919, was called "un-German," and its archives and library of 20,000 books were raided and burned as part of the huge, organized Nazi book burnings. Hirschfeld was violently assaulted on several occasions, but he managed to escape the Nazi terror, and he died in Paris in 1935.

In 1934, the Nazi secret police, the Gestapo, opened an "antigay" division to hunt down LGBTQ+ people, particularly gay men. In 1935 alone, 8,500 were arrested. The antigay laws that had been relaxed as a result of Hirschfeld's efforts were now tightened and made more punishing.

As the Nazi grip on Europe expanded, so too did the wave of antigay fanaticism. LGBTQ+ people hauled in for questioning were pressured to name others. Many gay men were sent to prison, while up to 15,000 were sent to concentration camps. It is impossible to know how many LGBTQ+ people perished in Germany's death camps, but what is well known is that they were often singled out for particular cruelty.

HAVE YOU HEARD OF?

Edward Carpenter (1844–1929)
An influential British writer and reformer, Carpenter declared his homosexuality was "perfectly natural."

Lettice Floyd (1865–1934)
This prominent British suffragette had an openly lesbian relationship with fellow suffragette Annie Williams.

Gladys Bentley (1907–1960)
This African American lesbian rose to fame as a cross-dressing entertainer in 1920s New York.

HOMOSEXUAL PRISONERS AT SACHSENHAUSEN
CONCENTRATION CAMP, GERMANY, IN 1938

THE PINK TRIANGLE

In the same way that the Nazis forced Jewish people to wear a yellow Star of David, gay men in the concentration camps were made to wear a downward-pointing pink triangle. Today, though, the pink triangle is no longer a badge of shame. It has been reclaimed by the LGBTQ+ community as a symbol of gay power and pride. In the 1980s, campaigners used the symbol to draw attention to the AIDS crisis facing gay men, and in the 1990s, a sign bearing a pink triangle within a green circle came to signify a safe space for LGBTQ+ people. Pink triangles are now proudly worn in gay rights demonstrations around the world.

MARLENE DIETRICH

1901–1992

A superstar of Hollywood's golden era, Marlene Dietrich was famed as much for wearing a top hat and tails as she was for being a femme fatale. She had relationships with both men and women, and never tried to hide her bisexuality, making her an icon for the LGBTQ+ community around the world.

Born Maria Magdalene Dietrich in Germany, she initially hoped to follow a career as a violinist. In her late teens, she began acting, landing small parts in theater productions and films. As her family disapproved of her acting, she combined her first and middle names to create a stage name.

In 1924, Dietrich married Rudolf Sieber, who worked in the film industry, and the couple had a daughter, Maria. The pair separated in 1929, though they remained married for fifty-two years, until Sieber's death in 1976. In 1930, Dietrich was catapulted to fame when she starred as Lola Lola, a nightclub dancer, in Germany's first talking picture, *Der Blaue Engle*. An English-language version of the film, *The Blue Angel,* made Dietrich a global star.

Dietrich moved to the US in 1930, where she was cast opposite Gary Cooper in *Morocco* as Amy Jolly, a lounge singer. The film is famous for a scene where Dietrich, dressed in a man's top hat and tuxedo, kisses a pretty lady who is watching the cabaret. Incredibly daring for the time, it marked the beginning of Dietrich's carefully crafted persona. Dressing in masculine clothes, both on- and off-screen, she challenged the accepted view of what a woman should be, and

her style had a big impact on fashion. Throughout the 1930s Dietrich starred in films such as *Shanghai Express* (1932), *The Devil Is a Woman* (1935), and *Destry Rides Again* (1939).

Dietrich was horrified by the rise of Adolf Hitler in Germany, and when she was asked to return to Berlin and perform in Nazi propaganda films, she flatly refused. In 1939, she renounced her German citizenship and became an American. During the Second World War, she made recordings intended to lower the morale of German soldiers and frequently performed near the front lines to entertain Allied troops. Dietrich was presented with the US Medal of Freedom in 1945.

In the years following the war, Dietrich starred in several more successful films, including *A Foreign Affair* (1948) and *Witness for the Prosecution* (1957). From the 1950s until the 1970s, she worked as a highly paid cabaret artist, performing to large audiences around the world. She lived her final years in Paris, dying at the age of ninety.

Throughout her life, Dietrich had many romantic affairs with leading Hollywood men such as Gary Cooper, John Gilbert, and Jimmy Stewart. She also had relationships with women, referring to them as her "sewing circle." These were rumored to include stars such as Greta Garbo, Dolores del Rio, and Barbara Stanwyck.

Perhaps the words of one of the twentieth century's most famous theater critics, Kenneth Tynan, best sums up the enigmatic appeal of Marlene Dietrich: "She has sex but no positive gender. Her masculinity appeals to women and her sexuality to men."

" I AM, AT HEART, A GENTLEMAN. "

MARLENE DIETRICH

WHY I HAVE PRIDE

Name

AYO BABATOPE

Age

22

Identifies as

QUEER

Having pride is about having a strong sense of self-worth and knowing who you are. It's being able to look past the social constructs society places on people, being able to love yourself enough that you can think beyond your immediate needs to be part of a bigger picture.

To me, Marsha P. Johnson is truly inspirational. Without her personal pride, global pride wouldn't exist. She demanded a response from the world. Can you imagine standing so proudly that your drive and determination can't be stopped by the beliefs of wider society?

There will always be people who choose to disagree with our sense of pride. They are unable to see our beauty and the power of love. But we all have to remember that taking pride in who we are can inspire people we don't even know are watching. There are vast numbers of people on this planet silently looking for permission to be themselves every day. So pride to me is about gently communicating to others, even if it's subconsciously, that it's okay to be yourself. I believe this is one of the greatest gifts you can give somebody.

Many times my first encounters with people involve them saying, "Thank you." Younger me couldn't comprehend why they were thanking me. However, now I realize that sometimes, as a queer person, you forget that merely existing is having pride. Just laughing is pride. You never know who is watching—it could be a young person who is being bullied for who they are, and seeing such authentic expression will resonate with them.

> ## WE CAN INSPIRE PEOPLE WE DON'T EVEN KNOW ARE WATCHING.

I have dedicated the last year of my life to myself. This has involved unlearning a lot of what I was taught while growing up in Lagos, Nigeria, a heavily religious society. I am also an "immigrant" in London, which has not been easy at times, but I am lucky and grateful to have met amazing people on my journey. I have taken up ballroom dancing, and this has made my self-confidence and sense of self attain new heights.

My biggest dream is to be able to communicate with others who identify similarly to me and let them know anything is possible. Anything you dream or want is possible. It may sound corny, but if you see it you can achieve it. I do my best to live a life of example, so even if you reading this is our only interaction, I hope you can take a sense of pride in who you are from my words.

TURNING
POINTS

The 1940s and 1950s were a dark period for the LGBTQ+ community. Although the Second World War (1939–1945) gave LGBTQ+ people more opportunities to meet each other, society was as intolerant and disapproving as ever.

The onset of the Cold War ushered in a new period of suspicion and persecution, and the 1950s saw a wave of antigay witch hunts. However, as Gertrude Stein famously said, "When you persecute people, you always rouse them to be strong and stronger." The seeds of a revolution were being planted.

SHAKING THINGS UP

Despite the horrors of Nazi oppression, the Second World War offered LGBTQ+ people opportunities to meet like-minded individuals and to discover, and even embrace, who they were. Millions of men and women were thrown together in all-male or all-female environments, far away from the watchful eyes of judgmental family or neighbors. In this atmosphere, LGBTQ+ connections flourished more easily. Although homosexuality was still illegal in most countries, the authorities were more likely to overlook it because their focus was on the war effort.

The war also turned gender roles upside down. With so many men away at war, women were permitted to take on roles traditionally filled by men, and in doing so they discovered a new sense of independence. In recruitment posters, women were shown looking strong and competent. And with men away from home, women relied more on each other for support, so sexual relationships were more likely to thrive.

After the war ended in 1945, life returned to normal in many ways. Men went back to their civilian jobs, women became housewives once again, and the witch hunts for LGBTQ+ people resumed. But something had changed. The sheer horror of the war had forced many people to think about society in a new way—there was a desire for a kinder, more tolerant world. Many of those who had found same-sex love were unwilling to return to their old lives, and they would play a part in the new organizations that were emerging.

> ❝ WOULDN'T IT BE WONDERFUL IF ALL OUR LETTERS COULD BE PUBLISHED IN THE FUTURE IN A MORE ENLIGHTENED TIME. THEN ALL THE WORLD COULD SEE HOW IN LOVE WE ARE. ❞
>
> LETTER FROM INFANTRYMAN GORDON BOWSHER TO GUNNER GILBERT BRADLEY DURING THE SECOND WORLD WAR, DISCOVERED IN 2008

CHRISTINE JORGENSEN (1926–1989)

Christine Jorgensen was America's first transgender celebrity. As a teenager, she felt trapped in the wrong body. After serving in the US army, she traveled to Denmark for hormone treatment and gender reassignment surgery. The American public was fascinated: "Ex-GI Becomes Blonde Beauty!" shouted one newspaper headline. Compared to the hostility that LGBTQ+ people usually received, Christine was treated with respect. She used her fame to raise trans awareness, and (in her own words) gave the sexual revolution "a good swift kick in the pants!"

After the Second World War, the LGBTQ+ cultures that had been silenced in Nazi Europe stirred again. Many new groups were founded in the late 1940s, like Denmark's Forbundet af 1948 ("League of 1948") and the COC ("Centre for Culture and Leisure") in the Netherlands, which is now the oldest active LGBTQ+ organization in the world. The word "homophile" came into use as an alternative to "homosexual," placing the emphasis on love rather than sex, and the groups that formed during this period became known as the homophile movement.

Meanwhile, in the US, two groundbreaking books by zoologist and biologist Dr. Alfred Kinsey were published. *Sexual Behavior in the Human Male* (1948) and *Sexual Behavior in the Human Female* (1953) claimed that far more people were gay, lesbian, or bisexual than anyone had ever suspected. The idea that 10 percent of the male population and up to 3 percent of women were mostly or completely homosexual caused public outrage, but the Kinsey Reports did have a positive impact on how some people thought about same-sex relationships.

Despite Kinsey's work, however, the so-called "Lavender Scare" was at work in 1950s America. The Cold War encouraged fear and suspicion—the "Red Scare" meant that anyone labeled as a Communist sympathizer was rooted out of government. In the same way, many LGBTQ+ people also lost their government posts and were prohibited from holding professional jobs.

In 1950, in this atmosphere of hatred and persecution, activist Harry Hay set up the Mattachine Society—a support group for gay and bisexual men. A few years later, lesbian couple Phyllis Lyon and Del Martin (who, in 2008, would become one of the first same-sex couples to legally marry in California) set up the Daughters of Bilitis—a secret society for lesbians and bisexual women. The name was based on a nineteenth-century collection of lesbian poetry, *The Songs of Bilitis*, so the society could pass as a poetry club. In 1956, it published the first issue of *The Ladder*—America's first lesbian newsletter.

PHYLLIS LYON AND DEL MARTIN GETTING MARRIED IN 2008

One famous member of the Daughters of Bilitis was the activist and playwright Lorraine Hansberry (1930–1965). She wrote the groundbreaking *A Raisin in the Sun*—the first play by an African American woman to open on Broadway. Although Hansberry never officially came out as a lesbian, she contributed to *The Ladder* under the initials LHN.

" I'M GLAD AS HECK YOU EXIST. "

LORRAINE HANSBERRY'S FIRST LETTER TO THE EDITORS OF *THE LADDER*

GIOVANNI'S ROOM

The celebrated African American writer James Baldwin (1924–1987) was born and raised in the New York neighborhood of Harlem. Desperate to escape the racism and homophobia that tainted life in the US, he moved to Paris, where his landmark novel *Giovanni's Room* was published in 1956. The book explores homosexuality, bisexuality, and social isolation with moving honesty. Its characters are interestingly all white—Baldwin later said that it was just too difficult to tackle the twin agonies of racism and the hatred of LGBTQ+ people in one story.

" EVERYBODY'S JOURNEY IS INDIVIDUAL. YOU DON'T KNOW WITH WHOM YOU'RE GOING TO FALL IN LOVE. . . . IF YOU FALL IN LOVE WITH A BOY, YOU FALL IN LOVE WITH A BOY. THE FACT THAT MANY AMERICANS CONSIDER IT A DISEASE SAYS MORE ABOUT THEM THAN IT DOES ABOUT HOMOSEXUALITY. "

JAMES BALDWIN, 1969

These days, it's hard for us to imagine how repressive the atmosphere was for the LGBTQ+ community in the 1950s. Laws varied from country to country, but even in places where homosexuality was legal, LGBTQ+ people felt the heavy burden of moral and social disapproval. Homosexuality was never a crime under Polish law, and it was decriminalized in Denmark (1933), Iceland (1940), Switzerland (1942), and Sweden (1944), but that did not make life easy for LGBTQ+ people.

> " HOMOSEXUAL BEHAVIOUR IN PRIVATE BETWEEN CONSENTING ADULTS SHOULD NO LONGER BE A CRIMINAL OFFENCE. "
> THE WOLFENDEN REPORT, 1957

Britain followed the US, clamping down on LGBTQ+ offenses and attempting to rid the government of homosexual influences. Undercover police officers posed as gay men in order to ensnare offenders, and in the early 1950s, up to one thousand men were jailed each year.

In 1953, the great British actor and theater director Sir John Gielgud was caught out by such a trap, and the details were splashed across the newspapers. Although Gielgud was only fined and not imprisoned, the experience led him to suffer a nervous breakdown a few months later.

In this sinister atmosphere of witch hunts, the British government feared that gay civil servants could easily be blackmailed into giving away state secrets. As a result, the Wolfenden Committee, led by Sir John Wolfenden, was set up to consider whether the law should be changed.

THE WOLFENDEN COMMITTEE

Over a period of three years, the committee interviewed gay men and met sixty-two times. Worried that female secretaries might be offended by the terms "homosexuals" and "prostitutes," the Wolfenden Committee members used the code "Huntley and Palmers"—a well-known brand of biscuits!

In 1957, a 155-page report concluded that homosexuality should not be a crime. As a result, the Homosexual Law Reform Society was set up in 1958. There was now light at the end of the tunnel—though it would be another nine years before the law actually changed in 1967 in England and Wales, a historic day for western civil rights.

ALAN TURING, WHO DIED BY
EATING A POISONED APPLE

André Gide (1869–1951)
A French writer who was the first openly gay man to receive the Nobel Prize for Literature in 1947.

Dawn Langley Simmons (c.1922–2000)
Born male, this colorful English writer had one of the first gender-reassignment operations in the US.

Allen Ginsberg (1926–1997)
This American poet, a core member of the "Beat Generation," refused to be quiet about his homosexuality.

ALAN TURING (1912–1954)

One of those who tragically fell victim to the 1950s antigay witch hunts was British mathematical genius Alan Turing. His work as a codebreaker during the Second World War played a huge role in the Allies' defeat of the Nazis. Yet, despite his status as a national hero, he was convicted of "gross indecency" for his relationship with a man in 1952. As an alternative to prison, Turing agreed to "chemical castration" treatment. His death, in 1954, is widely believed to have been a suicide. In 2013, Turing received a royal pardon.

AUDRE LORDE

1934–1992

Openly lesbian at a time when it was socially unacceptable, Lorde described herself as a "black, lesbian, feminist, mother, poet, warrior." Her writing covered everything from her sexuality to race, gender, feminism, and politics. She believed that people are complex and cannot conveniently be put into one "box"—and that many different identities shape our lives.

The youngest of three girls, Lorde was born in Harlem, New York, to West Indian parents. At school, she was the only Black student in her class, and she suffered awkwardness and isolation—feelings compounded by her being so short-sighted that she was legally blind.

At the age of twelve, Lorde began writing poetry. Her first poem, "Spring," was published in *Seventeen* magazine in 1951.

> **" IT IS NOT OUR DIFFERENCES THAT DIVIDE US. IT IS OUR INABILITY TO RECOGNIZE, ACCEPT AND CELEBRATE THOSE DIFFERENCES. "**
>
> AUDRE LORDE

As a teenager, she experienced crushes on female teachers and fellow students. Later, one of her poems, "From the House of Yemanjá," would capture her sense of not fitting in:

> **MY MOTHER HAD TWO FACES AND A FRYING POT**
> **WHERE SHE COOKED UP HER DAUGHTERS**
> **INTO GIRLS**
> **BEFORE SHE FIXED OUR DINNER.**
> **MY MOTHER HAD TWO FACES**
> **AND A BROKEN POT**
> **WHERE SHE HID OUT A PERFECT DAUGHTER**
> **WHO WAS NOT ME.**

After graduating, Lorde became a librarian and, despite her lesbian identity, married Edward Rollins. The couple had two children, but divorced in 1970. During this time, Lorde became a vocal participant in the civil rights movement.

Lorde began teaching poetry and fell in love with a woman called Frances Clayton, with whom she built a family life. In 1968, she published her first collection of poetry, *The First Cities*. A second volume, *Cables to Rage*, followed in 1970, in which she publicly came out in the poem "Martha." Lorde began to reach a wider audience and wrote essays and prose, tackling subjects that were important to her as a mother, a lesbian, a Black woman, and a feminist.

In 1978, Lorde fell ill with breast cancer, documenting her illness in *The Cancer Journals* (1980). She refused to see herself as a victim and wanted to celebrate herself—and all women—as a warrior. After battling the disease for more than a decade, she died at the age of fifty-eight.

Today, Lorde is celebrated as someone who saw her identity as a Black lesbian woman as central to who she was. Proud and unapologetic, she dared to be powerful. As she said, "We must recognize that difference is a reason for celebration and growth, rather than a reason for destruction." Her courageous writing has helped many other people to find the strength to be open about their identities, too.

WHY I HAVE PRIDE

Name
MUPELA MUMBA

Age
24

Identifies as
QUEER

Pride to me is being fearless. Being a young, Black, female queer in society today is an incredible, scary, and yet exciting experience, and you have to be completely fearless. Over the past few years I have been on an exploration of who I am and who I would like to be. It's difficult enough being a female in today's society—then there's being a Black female in society. And then there's being a Black queer female in society. That's a hard one to handle sometimes.

To be honest, from my personal experience, the LGBTQ+ community is not an easy one to navigate when you're first coming out as a person of color. Initially, I didn't find a connection or relate to the community because people like me were rarely in the spotlight. Only a very small part of our community was acknowledged. I am lucky now that I discovered and can share in UK Black Pride. It provided me with a light of hope, telling me that I am beautiful the way I am.

In all honesty, my mother, being African, had a tough time understanding when I came out. It's not easy for parents of a traditional ethnic background to understand. Remember to love yourself even more during this stage. As a Black female, coming out can be one of the most difficult stages in our lives. But we must stay strong and love ourselves harder than we ever have before.

> MY COMING OUT DIDN'T FEEL LIKE COMING OUT. IT FELT MORE LIKE I WAS ACCEPTING WHO I WAS BECOMING.

The story of Black queers is an important one: We started this Pride movement, yet we don't acknowledge that, or see that enough, in today's society. I think it's important to speak about it more and show that our pride truly does stand strong and shine.

Being a Black female and queer, and coming to terms with accepting myself as that, isn't always easy. There are times I doubt myself, but I know I'm still growing and I'm on a journey of self-discovery. Nothing is final: Life changes, we change, we grow and evolve. Titles fade, but our stories continue to develop. I have learned that nothing has to be certain right now. What's important is to enjoy life and live the change I want to see.

THE
BIRTH OF
PRIDE

On a hot, sultry night in June 1969, a historic event in the push for LGBTQ+ rights began: the Stonewall Riots. Many pioneers and groups had come together before this moment, but Stonewall marked the symbolic birth of an organized global movement.

Before the riots, protestors had struggled to be heard. Their tone was one of pleading rather than defiance. But now enough was enough. A spark had been ignited. Fury spilled onto the streets. And as confidence in the new movement grew, so too did something else—Pride.

FIGHTING BACK

The 1960s were a time of great political and social change in the western world. Young people began to question authority and rebel against the social conformity of the 1950s. There was a desire for more freedom and for more rights, both for women and for minority groups. In the US, the struggle for civil rights for African Americans gathered real momentum, and protests against the Vietnam War became a force of resistance.

For the LGBTQ+ community, the 1960s saw progress as well as setbacks. Hungary decriminalized homosexuality in 1961, while Illinois became the first state in the US to do so in 1962. In the UK, although the Sexual Offences Act of 1967 was a step in the right direction—making homosexuality legal for men aged over twenty-one in England and Wales—it didn't fully decriminalize sexual acts between men. Furthermore, the Roman Catholic Church stated in 1961 that those "affected by the perverse inclination" of homosexuality should not be permitted to take religious vows or be ordained. It was clear that society continued to regard LGBTQ+ people with contempt and that decriminalization didn't mean instant change.

In 1966, three years before the Stonewall Riots, the Mattachine Society staged a small but important protest. At the time, many New York bars refused to serve gay people because of a regulation introduced by the State Liquor Authority, which flagged homosexual patrons as being potentially "disorderly." On April 21, three Mattachine members, accompanied by news reporters, entered a popular bar. They explained to the bartender that they were gay, before ordering drinks and waiting to be refused service. The story hit the newspapers, shining a light on the routine harassment suffered by LGBTQ+ people. The protest became known as the "Sip-in" and led to the New York City Commission on Human Rights declaring that gay people had a right to be served. This small act of resistance showed that change was possible. The stage had been set for a greater protest.

BAYARD RUSTIN (1912–1987)

Bayard Rustin experienced discrimination and prejudice twice over—as a Black man and as a gay man. He was a key figure in the American civil rights movement, but because of his sexuality, his name was not widely known. Born into a Quaker family, he believed in nonviolent protest, and in the 1950s became a mentor to Martin Luther King Jr. Rustin lived an openly gay life, and some civil rights leaders feared his sexuality would discredit their cause—so he was kept behind the scenes. Few people realized Rustin was the brilliant mastermind who orchestrated the 1963 March on Washington—the civil rights event where Martin Luther King Jr. made his famous "I Have a Dream" speech.

BAYARD RUSTIN

"IT WAS AN ABSOLUTE NECESSITY FOR ME TO DECLARE HOMOSEXUALITY, BECAUSE IF I DIDN'T I WAS A PART OF THE PREJUDICE."

BAYARD RUSTIN

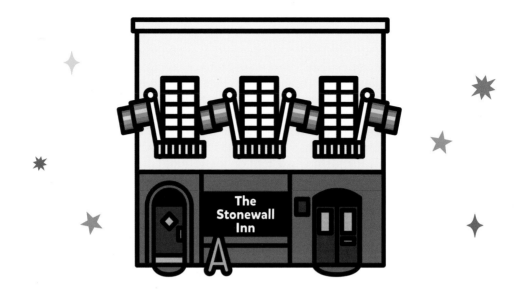

The Stonewall Inn was a bar in New York's Greenwich Village where gay men, lesbians, transgender people, and drag queens could relax and openly express themselves. At the time, it was very difficult for the LGBTQ+ community to do this—remember that even a man holding another man's hand in public could result in a prison sentence.

The New York police regularly raided gay bars looking for reasons to close them down. In the early hours of June 28, 1969, they raided the Stonewall Inn. The same thing had happened just three days earlier, and people were fed up with accepting this constant harassment. As usual, the police roughly pushed customers around and demanded to see their IDs. But things didn't go as planned for the police that night, and events quickly got out of hand. As handcuffed customers were shoved outside and bundled into vans, a growing crowd began to throw objects at the police.

HAVE YOU HEARD OF?

José Sarria (1922–2013)
This drag performer and activist became the first openly gay American to run for political office in 1961.

Rita Mae Brown (born 1944)
An activist, feminist, and author of the 1973 novel *Rubyfruit Jungle*, which shocked the world with its frank lesbian portrayal.

Ted Brown (born 1950)
An American-born British activist and member of the GLF, he founded Black Lesbians and Gays Against Media Homophobia.

Accounts vary as to what part the different members of the LGBTQ+ community played, but some say that when a Black lesbian called Stormé DeLarverie was thrown into a van, she yelled at bystanders to do something. Anger quickly spread and the crowd violently erupted: Police vans were rocked, tires were slashed, and bottles and rocks were thrown at the police, who ended up barricading themselves into the Stonewall Inn.

The police were rescued by reinforcements that night, but it was not the end of the Stonewall uprising. For six more days and nights, people took to the streets in protest against police oppression and brutality. There was no turning back now: The LGBTQ+ community demanded equality.

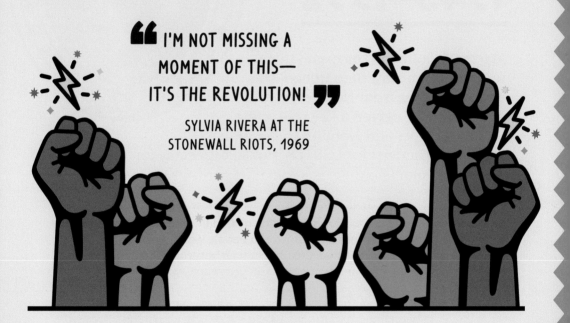

"I'M NOT MISSING A MOMENT OF THIS—IT'S THE REVOLUTION!"

SYLVIA RIVERA AT THE STONEWALL RIOTS, 1969

SYLVIA RIVERA (1951–2002)

Sylvia Rivera, a Latin-American drag queen who helped mobilize the crowd at the Stonewall Riots, worked tirelessly for transgender rights. Sylvia had had a troubled childhood and had lived on the streets from the age of eleven until she was taken in by a group of drag queens. After the Stonewall Riots, she joined the newly formed Gay Liberation Front (GLF) and cofounded STAR (Street Transvestite Action Revolutionaries) with her friend Marsha P. Johnson. Rivera's harsh life experiences gave her real empathy for those living on the margins of society. At the time, trans people struggled to find acceptance, even within the LGBTQ+ community.

MARSHA P. JOHNSON

1945–1992

Marsha P. Johnson once said that until she became a drag queen, she was a "nobody, from Nowheresville." This "nobody" played a key role at the Stonewall Riots and went on to become a trailblazing activist for LGBTQ+ rights, especially for people of color.

Johnson began trying on dresses around the age of five, but was punished when she was caught. After high school, she moved to Greenwich Village in New York, where she became a sex worker to survive. She found a sense of family amongst the city's drag queens, and in time became a "drag mother," offering support to young and homeless LGBTQ+ people.

Johnson loved wearing outrageous hats and lots of jewelery. When asked what the "P" in her name stood for, she would retort, "Pay it no mind!" If asked about her gender, she would give the same response—at the time, the word "transgender" was not in use, and she didn't like labels.

Johnson and her close friend Sylvia Rivera became well-known drag queens in Greenwich Village. Accounts of the Stonewall Riots vary, but eyewitnesses have said that Johnson and Rivera were both at the forefront of the uprising. After the riots, Johnson joined the Gay Liberation Front (GLF) and was actively involved in organizing protests. Together with Rivera, she founded STAR (Street Transvestite Action Revolutionaries) and opened a house for young, homeless trans people.

When the AIDS crisis tore through the heart of the LGBTQ+ community in the 1980s, Johnson became an active fundraiser and marched with the group ACT UP to raise awareness.

Alongside her activism, Johnson was also a member of a drag performance troupe called the Hot Peaches that regularly performed in New York and did a tour in London. In 1975, the artist Andy Warhol made her the subject of one of his silkscreen portraits.

To her friends, Johnson was known for her spirited, generous nature, but she also suffered poor mental health, and at times was hospitalized. Her death, at the age of forty-six, has never been fully explained. Her body was tragically found in the Hudson River in 1992, and although it was ruled a suicide, many of her friends strongly believed she was murdered.

Johnson never shied away from fighting for what she believed was right. As someone who understood what it was to feel like a "nobody," she fought courageously to make the world a safer, more welcoming place for vulnerable trans people. Her contribution to the gay liberation movement has not always been fully recognized. However, in 2019, it was announced that a monument would be unveiled near the site of the Stonewall Inn to honor Johnson and Rivera's bravery and commitment in the fight for transgender rights.

> **" HOW MANY YEARS HAS IT TAKEN FOR PEOPLE TO REALIZE THAT WE'RE ALL BROTHERS AND SISTERS AND HUMAN BEINGS AND IN THE HUMAN RACE? I MEAN HOW MANY YEARS DOES IT TAKE FOR PEOPLE TO SEE THAT? THAT WE'RE ALL IN THE RAT RACE TOGETHER! "**
>
> MARSHA P. JOHNSON

SAY IT LOUD

The Stonewall Riots made one thing clear. Nothing could be changed without action, and LGBTQ+ activists would need to become more organized, more visible, and a lot louder. In the years immediately following the riots, there was a sense of hope as a global movement took shape.

Immediately after the riots, the Gay Liberation Front (GLF) was formed in the US, calling for the sexual liberation of all people. It published a newspaper called *Come Out!* and organized meetings and demonstrations. A British branch of the GLF was formed in late 1970. It staged "gay days," festivals, and protests, and attracted high-profile media attention.

   Although the GLF later splintered into other groups, it set the agenda for what was needed: confrontation and direct action. Before 1970, few LGBTQ+ people had the courage to come out openly or to campaign publicly. They feared being disowned by their families, losing their jobs, or being arrested. Now there was a call to find strength in numbers, to be unafraid, and to take to the streets.

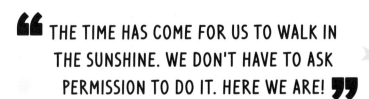

> ❝ THE TIME HAS COME FOR US TO WALK IN THE SUNSHINE. WE DON'T HAVE TO ASK PERMISSION TO DO IT. HERE WE ARE! ❞
>
> ACTIVIST MARTHA SHELLEY, ADDRESSING A GAY POWER VIGIL IN NEW YORK, JULY 1969

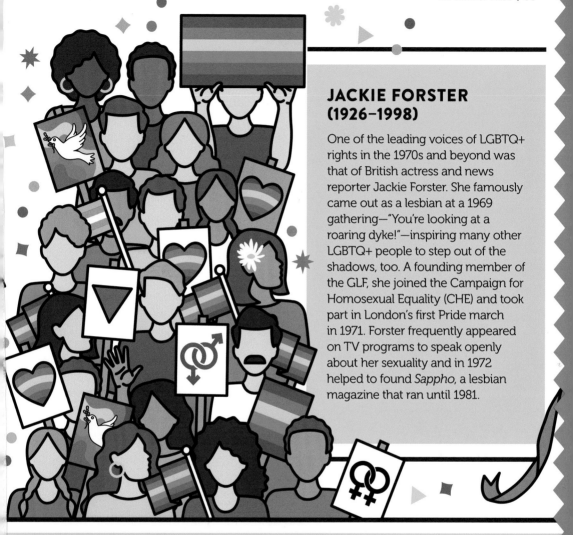

JACKIE FORSTER (1926–1998)

One of the leading voices of LGBTQ+ rights in the 1970s and beyond was that of British actress and news reporter Jackie Forster. She famously came out as a lesbian at a 1969 gathering—"You're looking at a roaring dyke!"—inspiring many other LGBTQ+ people to step out of the shadows, too. A founding member of the GLF, she joined the Campaign for Homosexual Equality (CHE) and took part in London's first Pride march in 1971. Forster frequently appeared on TV programs to speak openly about her sexuality and in 1972 helped to found *Sappho*, a lesbian magazine that ran until 1981.

NOT BAD, NOT MAD

In 1973, the Australian Medical Association changed its official view of homosexuality, no longer classing it as a mental illness or disorder. Two months later, the American Psychiatric Association followed suit. This was a landmark victory for LGBTQ+ rights, and it helped to change attitudes. However, it was not until 2019 that being transgender was dropped from the World Health Organization's (WHO) list of mental disorders.

Brenda Howard (1946–2005), a bisexual activist, was heavily involved in organizing New York's first LGBTQ+ "liberation" march in 1970. The slogan "Pride" was coined, and Howard became known as the "Mother of Pride." The idea quickly spread around the world—London held its first Pride march in 1972, Italy in 1978, and Germany and Spain in 1979.

" SAY IT LOUD, GAY IS PROUD! "

OFFICIAL CHANT FOR NEW YORK'S FIRST PRIDE MARCH

In Sydney, Australia, a parade was held in honor of the Stonewall Riots in June 1978, but it was violently halted by the police, who arrested many participants. As a result of this ugly episode, Australia relaxed its anti-LGBTQ+ laws. Since 1980, a huge Mardi Gras street party has been held in Sydney, and it's now one of the biggest and most colorful "Prides" in the world.

PETER TATCHELL (BORN 1952)

Australian-born Peter Tatchell has been at the forefront of the fight for LGBTQ+ rights for nearly five decades. He was a leading member of the Gay Liberation Front, helping to organize London's first Pride march in 1972. In 1973, he staged a protest in Communist East Germany, which saw him interrogated by the Stasi secret police. Tatchell was a leading member of the direct-action group OutRage! before founding the Peter Tatchell Foundation, which advocates for human rights and global democracy. In 2007, he was brutally attacked by neo-Nazis while marching at a banned Pride march in Moscow.

Thousands of Pride events now take place around the world each year. Pride—the opposite of shame—affirms the right of LGBTQ+ people to have equality and visibility, and to be treated with dignity. These days, Prides are rarely controversial in the western world, but that is certainly not the case in many countries. In recent years, tear gas and rubber bullets have been used against marchers in Istanbul, Turkey. In Russia, Moscow Pride began in 2006, but marches there have consistently been marred by violent attacks. In 2012, the Moscow courts banned Pride marches for the next one hundred years.

> **WE GOT MIXED REACTIONS FROM THE PUBLIC. SOME WERE HOSTILE. MANY WERE CURIOUS OR BEWILDERED. MOST HAD NEVER KNOWINGLY SEEN A GAY PERSON, LET ALONE HUNDREDS OF QUEERS MARCHING TO DEMAND FREEDOM.**
>
> PETER TATCHELL, DESCRIBING LONDON'S FIRST OFFICIAL PRIDE MARCH IN 1972

THE RAINBOW FLAG

In 1977, Harvey Milk, one of the first openly gay people to be elected to political office in the US, asked Gilbert Baker to create a symbol for the gay community—and the Rainbow Flag was born. Initially the flag had eight stripes, but in time two were dropped (pink for sexuality and turquoise for magic). This left six stripes:

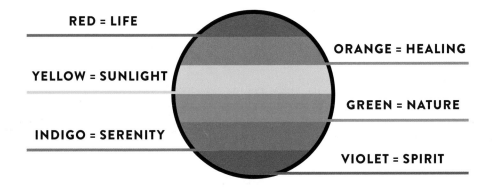

RED = LIFE

ORANGE = HEALING

YELLOW = SUNLIGHT

GREEN = NATURE

INDIGO = SERENITY

VIOLET = SPIRIT

HARVEY MILK

1930–1978

At a time when many LGBTQ+ people experienced daily hatred and discrimination, the election to political office of Harvey Milk—an openly gay man and human-rights champion—was a beacon of hope. He was tragically assassinated, but his dream of an equal society has never died.

Born in New York, Milk was a popular boy who enjoyed sports and opera. As a teenager, he was increasingly aware of his attraction to other boys, but he kept it private. After earning a teaching degree in 1951, Milk joined the US navy during the Korean War, reaching the rank of junior lieutenant. In 1955, he returned to New York and worked in many different roles, including in teaching, the theater, and investment banking. He was now pursuing gay relationships, but he initially kept his public and private lives separate.

Through his theater work, Milk was introduced to a highly visible gay culture, and he began to move away from his conservative values, embracing his sexuality and leaning to the left in his political views.

Milk moved to San Francisco in 1972 with his partner, Scott Smith, where he opened a camera shop called Castro Cameras. There was a thriving gay community in the city, but it faced constant police harassment—and Milk soon found his voice as an LGBTQ+ activist and community leader.

In 1973, Milk entered the race to be elected to the San Francisco Board of Supervisors. An inspiring public speaker, he was able to fire up crowds, but with

> **"ON THIS ANNIVERSARY OF STONEWALL, I ASK MY GAY SISTERS AND BROTHERS TO MAKE THE COMMITMENT TO FIGHT. WE WILL NOT WIN OUR RIGHTS BY STAYING QUIETLY IN OUR CLOSETS. "**
>
> SPEECH AT THE SAN FRANCISCO PRIDE PARADE, 1978

little political experience or funding, he lost the election. By his third attempt, however, Milk had gained valuable experience and an army of supporters, and he finally won a seat in 1977.

Once in office, Milk worked with the liberal mayor, George Moscone. Moscone had succeeded in reducing the scope of the city's anti-sodomy law and had overseen the appointment of several LGBTQ+ people to the board.

But someone was not happy about Milk's success. Dan White, a Vietnam veteran, was a board supervisor who had become increasingly bitter at what he saw as the breakdown of traditional values. After resigning from his post, he decided he wanted his job back a few days later—but was refused. Seeking revenge, he crept through an open window of City Hall and shot Mayor Moscone, and then Milk, dead.

That evening, thousands of people marched through the city and held a candlelight vigil. There was a feeling that out of respect for Milk's values, violence should not be the response. However, when Dan White was found guilty of manslaughter rather than murder, the LGBTQ+ community erupted in anger, and there were riots. White served five years of his seven-year sentence, but took his own life soon after his release.

Today, Harvey Milk is remembered as someone who bravely forged a path to public office in the face of discrimination and danger—an achievement that must have seemed impossible when he was starting out. In doing so, he helped many LGBTQ+ people to find the strength to step out of the closet, to tell the truth, and to break down what he called the "conspiracy of silence."

HARVEY MILK

PRIDES
AROUND THE WORLD

More than fifty years on from the Stonewall Riots, over two hundred parades, parties, and rallies take place around the world each year. Prides have spread to every continent, but in some countries, participants still risk abuse and even state brutality.

NEW YORK, UNITED STATES

More than two thousand people marched to Central Park in New York's first Pride March on June 28, 1970, held a year after the Stonewall Riots. It was called Christopher Street Liberation Day, named after the road where the Stonewall Inn was located. In 2019, more than 4 million people took part in the dazzling street party that marked fifty years since the Stonewall Riots.

JOHANNESBURG, SOUTH AFRICA

The first Pride march in South Africa—and on the African continent—was held in Johannesburg in 1990. Today, Johannesburg's "Pride of Africa" remains the biggest LGBTQ+ event in Africa—a continent notorious for its widespread antigay laws.

SHANGHAI, CHINA

In 2009, Shanghai became the first Chinese city to hold a Pride event. Although small by western standards, it's one of the fastest-growing Prides in Asia, and it aims to raise awareness of issues like China's lack of marriage equality.

TORONTO, CANADA

First formed in 1971, Pride Toronto is one of the world's biggest and most diverse Pride parties. Now running throughout the month of June, the event includes a Dyke March and a Trans Pride as well as a Pride Parade.

THE GOVERNMENT HAS CLAMPED DOWN ON PRIDE IN UGANDA.

UGANDA

In Uganda, homosexuality is illegal—and in 2019 the government called for the death penalty to be reintroduced for same-sex acts. Nevertheless, the first Pride was held in 2014. However, a brutal crackdown on events in 2016 and 2017 has made holding further Prides too dangerous for the time being.

TEL AVIV, ISRAEL

The biggest LGBTQ+ event in the Middle East, Tel Aviv Pride is a week-long celebration famous for its round-the-clock parties. First held in 1993, the event now draws more than 200,000 revelers.

SÃO PAULO, BRAZIL

Attracting well over 4 million people each year, São Paulo is home to the largest and one of the most colorful Prides in the world. Despite this, Brazil has one of the world's highest rates of LGBTQ+ hate crime, especially directed against the transgender community.

A HUGE RAINBOW FLAG IS CARRIED AT SÃO PAULO PRIDE.

MADRID, SPAIN

Europe's largest Pride turns Madrid's city center into one huge party, with more than 2 million revelers. Outdoor concerts and cabarets and a flamboyant parade make this one of the best Prides in the world.

WHY I HAVE PRIDE

Name

SHELINA

Age

26

Identifies as

LESBIAN

I was born and brought up in East London, the hub of the city's Bengali community. I first realized I was a lesbian during secondary school. However I had to push it to the back of my mind. Back then, I was fearful of what coming out would do for me. It is a difficult process, especially when you're a teenager and your hormones are all over the place. You feel quite alone and start to withdraw yourself from others because you feel like an imposter.

Now, I am out to immediate family, close friends, and colleagues. Bizarrely, I've found that the workplace environment is the most nonjudgmental of them all. I can be who I am with no questions asked, although I am unsure if this is because you cannot discriminate openly against others at work, or because my colleagues are genuinely accepting.

When I came out to my family it didn't go down well, but that is to be expected. I am working on those relationships. I have also lost friends over my sexuality, but I see it as a blessing if I lose friends once I come out to them—it tells me they were never really my friends!

I would say the main difficulty I face being a lesbian and a Muslim would be dealing with my intersectionality as a Muslim and Person of Color. That can get quite mentally exhausting. There is an identity crisis at all levels. I still question it today, and that is something that I am working on.

> YOU CAN RECONCILE BEING A LESBIAN AND BEING A MUSLIM. IT ISN'T MUTUALLY EXCLUSIVE. YOU CAN EXIST AND I AM LIVING PROOF OF IT.

However, there are also many positives. Some of my closest friends are LGBTQ+ Muslims, and that's what keeps me positive—that there are others out there like me.

I think that attitudes toward LGBTQ+ Muslims are changing. There are supportive charities and groups around the world now, whereas twenty years ago there were hardly any. I'd like to think that in the next twenty years, there will be no need for support groups as, Insha'Allah, being an LGBTQ+ Muslim won't be an issue anymore.

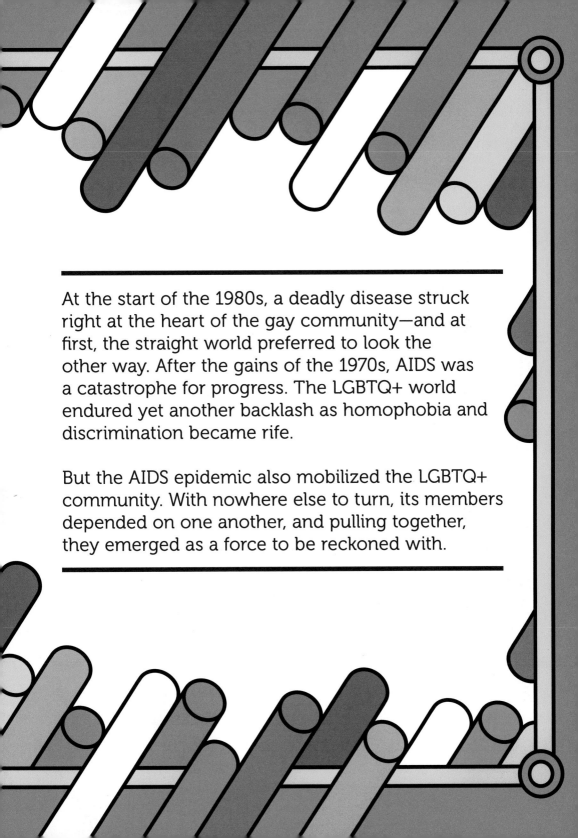

At the start of the 1980s, a deadly disease struck right at the heart of the gay community—and at first, the straight world preferred to look the other way. After the gains of the 1970s, AIDS was a catastrophe for progress. The LGBTQ+ world endured yet another backlash as homophobia and discrimination became rife.

But the AIDS epidemic also mobilized the LGBTQ+ community. With nowhere else to turn, its members depended on one another, and pulling together, they emerged as a force to be reckoned with.

FEAR AND LOATHING

For decades, LGBTQ+ people had been forced to endure society's misguided belief that homosexuality was an illness, but in the early 1980s a real disease hit the community hard.

HIV (human immunodeficiency virus) is a virus that attacks the body's immune system, making it less able to fight off infections. AIDS (acquired immunodeficiency syndrome) is the most advanced stage of HIV infection. Although there is no cure for HIV, people diagnosed with the condition today can take medication that allows them to lead healthy lives. However, in the 1980s and for most of the 1990s, HIV was almost always a death sentence.

Anyone can get HIV, but when it first arrived in westernized countries, it spread fastest among gay men. Most commonly, it's transmitted through unprotected sex or by sharing drug-injection needles. It cannot be transmitted through casual contact, such as kissing or sharing eating utensils.

Researchers believe that HIV originated in central Africa, around 1920. It's not certain when the virus first entered the US, but in 1981 there were several reports of previously healthy gay men mysteriously falling ill with rare infections. By the end of that year, there had been well over one hundred deaths in the US. As unease rapidly spread, the disease began to show itself around the world. Terrence Higgins was one of the first British people to die of the condition. After his death in July 1982, his family and friends set up the Terrence Higgins Trust—a charity that has been at the forefront of fighting HIV/AIDS ever since.

By 1984, scientists had worked out the cause of AIDS. Although the virus can infect anybody, fear and suspicion meant the LGBTQ+ community was isolated and victimized. Around the world, news headlines like "Gay Plague Brings Havoc" only stoked this prejudice.

ROCK HUDSON (1925–1985)

Hollywood legend Rock Hudson shocked the world when he announced he had AIDS in 1985. Just eleven weeks later, he was dead. The actor had hidden his HIV diagnosis for a year, but was compelled to come out of the closet because of rumors about his dramatic weight loss. Although Hudson's sexuality was an open secret in Hollywood, his image as a heterosexual "real" American man—tall, muscular, and handsome—had been successfully marketed to the public for decades. His death did much to raise awareness of AIDS. He left $250,000 to set up an AIDS research foundation, and his friend actress Elizabeth Taylor was inspired to become a prominent AIDS activist.

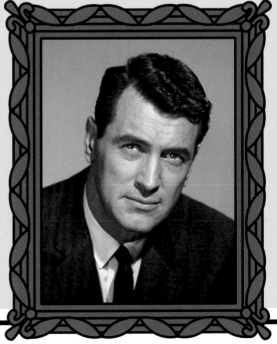

By 1987, there were 40,000 people with HIV in the US, but the administration was slow to act. President Reagan didn't publicly speak about AIDS until 1987, and funding for research was woefully inadequate. This was partly due to the perception that AIDS was a "gay problem."

Meanwhile, celebrity deaths around the world continued to draw attention to the devastating impact of AIDS. They included French philosopher Michel Foucault (1984), American supermodel Gia Carangi (1986), American pianist Liberace (1987), British rock star Freddie Mercury (1991), Russian ballet dancer Rudolf Nureyev (1993), American tennis player Arthur Ashe (1993), and Australian designer Leigh Bowery (1994).

In 1987, Princess Diana did much to challenge attitudes when she shook hands with a man dying from AIDS. Since it was still widely believed that just touching someone with the virus was risky, Princess Diana's simple gesture had a powerful impact.

Meanwhile, American activist Larry Kramer cofounded a direct-action group called ACT UP (AIDS Coalition to Unleash Power) in 1987. Its mission was to stage ambitious protests that would force government agencies and drug companies to take action. ACT UP became an international force, with a particularly strong presence in Paris. French activists staged "die-ins" and threw fake blood at medical researchers.

> **ACT UP HAS TAUGHT EVERYONE THAT YOU DON'T GET ANYTHING BY BEING NICE, GOOD LITTLE BOYS AND GIRLS. YOU DO NOT GET MORE WITH HONEY RATHER THAN VINEGAR.**
>
> LARRY KRAMER, AIDS ACTIVIST

HAVE YOU HEARD OF?

Cecilia Chung (born 1965)
An AIDS activist from Hong Kong who founded Positively Trans, a network for trans people living with HIV.

Magic Johnson (born 1959)
A US basketball star who announced he was HIV positive in 1991, helping to show AIDS was not a "gay disease."

Pedro Zamora (1972–1994)
A Cuban-American TV personality who appeared on the reality TV show *The Real World* as a gay man with AIDS.

The epidemic could no longer be ignored, but it was not until 1996 that an effective treatment for HIV became available. By then 6.4 million people had died, and more than 22 million were estimated to be living with the virus.

The AIDS crisis ripped through the heart of the gay community. So many died, and those left behind were traumatized and fearful for their own health. Added to this, people had to put up with a renewed wave of homophobia. But AIDS also brought different parts of the LGBTQ+ population together. Many lesbians played a crucial role by starting food banks and caring for the sick. United by tragedy, the LGBTQ+ community emerged as a strong political force.

ACT UP DEMONSTRATING AT THE
1988 NEW YORK PRIDE MARCH

RYAN WHITE (1971–1990)

At the age of thirteen, American schoolboy Ryan White was diagnosed with AIDS and given six months to live. A hemophiliac, Ryan had contracted HIV from a contaminated blood transfusion. Ryan was met with fear and hatred in his own community, and his school tried to ban him. The ensuing legal battle brought Ryan international fame, and he used the remaining five years of his life to battle the stigma faced by people with AIDS and to educate the public about how the virus is (and isn't) spread.

VITO RUSSO

1946–1990

Italian-American activist Vito Russo had fought for LGBTQ+ rights in the dark years before the Stonewall Riots and then all through the 1970s, but he truly found his voice during the AIDS crisis. When he, too, developed AIDS, he told people that he wasn't dying from it. As he said, "If I'm dying from anything, I'm dying from homophobia."

Born in Harlem, New York, Vito Russo knew from a young age that he was different, and he embraced that difference: "I never once, not for a second, believed that it was wrong to be gay, that it was a sin."

After Stonewall, Russo became a member of the Gay Activists Alliance (GAA) and was a founding member of the Gay & Lesbian Alliance Against Defamation (GLAAD), which monitors how LGBTQ+ people are portrayed in the media. Beyond his activism, Russo was a passionate movie fan, and he began researching how "queerness" was portrayed in films. He noticed that after 1930 (and the Hays Code, see page 36), whenever LGBTQ+ themes were present in film, there was negativity and misinformation. Not only was the general public exposed to this kind of propaganda, but it also affected the way gay people felt about themselves. As Russo said, "The first time I ever saw a gay character on the screen I was in high school . . . and he slit his throat in the end, and I took that home with me."

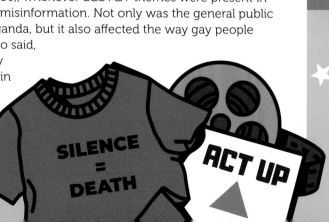

SILENCE = DEATH

ACT UP

Russo was determined to show people that such damaging portrayals were at the root of society's homophobia. Throughout the 1970s, he toured the US giving lecture presentations and film screenings. His groundbreaking book, *The Celluloid Closet*, was published in 1981.

In 1983, Russo cocreated and presented the first news show for the LGBTQ+ community, called *Our Time*. He was also instrumental in founding the direct-action group ACT UP and was one of the most outspoken activists in the fight against HIV/AIDS.

Russo lost many friends to HIV, including his partner Jeffrey Sevcik. In 1989, he appeared in the award-winning film *Common Threads: Stories from the Quilt*, in which he and others starkly discussed their grief and fury at the deaths of their loved ones. Russo received an HIV diagnosis himself in 1985, but even though it slowly robbed him of his health, he never gave up fighting. He continued to attend rallies and speak out until his death at the age of forty-four in 1990.

Today, Vito Russo is remembered as someone who was never afraid to challenge the status quo. As a gay man who fully embraced his identity, he turned his convictions into positive, inspiring actions. His work showed people how their prejudices were fueled by negative stereotypes. His anger at the lack of government action during the AIDS crisis made him a passionate and outspoken activist.

> **" SOMEDAY, THE AIDS CRISIS WILL BE OVER ... AND ... THERE'LL BE PEOPLE ALIVE ON THIS EARTH—GAY PEOPLE AND STRAIGHT PEOPLE, MEN AND WOMEN, BLACK AND WHITE—WHO WILL HEAR THE STORY THAT ONCE THERE WAS A TERRIBLE DISEASE ... AND THAT A BRAVE GROUP OF PEOPLE STOOD UP AND FOUGHT AND, IN SOME CASES, GAVE THEIR LIVES, SO THAT OTHER PEOPLE MIGHT LIVE AND BE FREE. "**
>
> VITO RUSSO ADDRESSING A CROWD AT AN ACT UP DEMONSTRATION IN WASHINGTON, DC, IN 1988

WHY I HAVE PRIDE

Name

ALEX HOLDSWORTH

Age

23

Identifies as

GAY

Pride can be defined as "confidence and self-respect as expressed by members of a group, typically one that has been socially marginalized, on the basis of their shared identity, culture, and experience." The key word in this definition that stands out to me is "confidence." When I look back at the confused teenager I was at school, I now realize it was a serious lack of confidence in myself that held me back. However, this was not the standard type of confidence that makes you nervous when publicly speaking; it was something else.

The further I went through school, the more this lack of confidence became an issue, and it even toyed with my mental health in sixth form [the last two years of secondary education in British schools]. Even though I was an outgoing individual, something never felt quite right. While everyone else found love a natural thing, it never seemed to click for me. I saw how happy everyone else was talking to their crushes, freely dating and even starting relationships. I attempted to do this myself by dating girls, but I always felt I was doing it more to fit into social norms and receive attention—which is the complete opposite of pride in my opinion.

It took going to university to realize what pride truly was. There were no limitations on who you could date or how you should act. You were actively encouraged to be the person you wanted to be. Most importantly you were judged on how kind you were as an individual and not by trivial factors such as your sexual orientation.

> **FOR THE FIRST TIME IN MY LIFE I SAW INDIVIDUALS BEING ABLE TO EXPRESS THEMSELVES IN ANY WAY THEY WANTED TO.**

As I went to university far from home, I had a fantastic opportunity to reinvent myself in a fresh social scene where no one knew my past. One night I had a long think about what I wanted to change about myself so as to become a happier person. It was that evening that I realized an individual must also have "self-respect" to be a complete person. Self-respect combined with confidence makes a person proud to be who they are.

Shortly after this I went on my first gay date, and for the first time in my life, I felt I had the inner confidence I had been craving and the "self-respect" I deserved. For the first time in my life, I had pride, and I could not be happier.

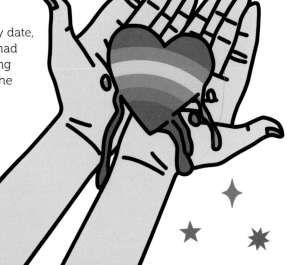

OUT
OF THE
SHADOWS

The AIDS crisis was a hammer blow for the LGBTQ+ community, giving rise to a new wave of persecution and oppression. But it also brought real anger, galvanizing people to pull together and agitate for lasting change. As more and more individuals in the public eye chose to step out of the shadows and embrace their sexual identity—including celebrities, sports stars, and politicians—the LGBTQ+ community braced itself for another battle: the push for marriage equality.

SETBACKS AND GAINS

AIDS not only devastated the gay community, it also fueled a vicious backlash. Homophobic messages spread by right-wing groups and a hostile media had a disastrous effect on public opinion.

For example, American pastor Jerry Falwell proclaimed, "AIDS is not just God's punishment for homosexuals, it is God's punishment for the society that tolerates homosexuals."

In Great Britain, Prime Minister Margaret Thatcher's Conservative government passed a law in 1988 known as Section 28. The first homophobic British law in more than one hundred years, it had a devastating impact on young LGBTQ+ people for years to come. Section 28 stated that local government could not intentionally "promote homosexuality." This meant that teachers felt unable to even mention LGBTQ+ issues or tackle homophobic bullying, libraries could not stock material with gay or lesbian themes, and there was no proper funding for LGBTQ+ support services for young people.

Campaigners reacted furiously. Lesbian activists rappelled into the House of Lords chamber from a viewing gallery, while a BBC news broadcast was disrupted by four lesbians handcuffing themselves to a TV camera. More than 20,000 protestors marched in Manchester, and actor Sir Ian McKellen came out as gay in order to voice his fury.

Section 28 jolted the LGBTQ+ movement into real fighting mode. Groups like Stonewall and OutRage! were founded, while Schools OUT UK (a charity set up as the Gay Teachers Association in 1974) worked tirelessly to keep LGBTQ+ issues visible.

Section 28 was finally removed from law in 2003, but its cruel legacy was far-reaching. Many LGBTQ+ children who grew up in its shadow were victimized, bullied, and forced to suffer in silence in schools that could offer neither support nor understanding.

MARGARET THATCHER LOUDLY VOICED HER OPPOSITION TO LGBTQ+ RIGHTS.

TROUBLE IN THE CLASSROOM

In 1983, a children's book called *Jenny Lives with Eric and Martin* by Danish author Susanne Bösche was published in English. The story, about a girl living with her father and his male partner, was intended to teach children about different family groupings. The media responded with outrage: "Vile Book in School!" screamed one headline. The education secretary described the book as "homosexual propaganda," while Margaret Thatcher stated, "Children . . . are being taught that they have an inalienable right to be gay." It was in this dark atmosphere that Section 28 was born.

" WE TALK ABOUT FAKE NEWS NOW, WHAT WE WERE SEEING THEN WAS DOWNRIGHT LIES. IF YOU WERE FOUND TO BE LESBIAN OR GAY AND A TEACHER, THE CHANCES WERE YOU'D BE SACKED. "

SUE SANDERS, CHAIR OF SCHOOLS OUT UK, TEACHER AND PROTESTOR AGAINST SECTION 28

As LGBTQ+ rights in Britain and the US appeared to take a backward step in the 1980s, there was some positive news elsewhere. In 1989, Denmark became the first country to pass a law allowing same-sex unions, calling them "registered partnerships." Norway and Sweden followed suit in 1993 and 1995 respectively.

In 1996, South Africa became the first country in the world to introduce equal rights for gay and lesbian people into its constitution. This meant that discrimination on the basis of race, gender, or sexual orientation was unlawful. Sadly this did not stamp out discrimination in South Africa. Hate crime, particularly against lesbian women, is still a big problem in rural areas.

There was a steep rise in hate crimes directed against the community as LGBTQ+ issues became more visible and politicized. In Britain, a series of unsolved murders of gay men included the savage killing of actor Michael Boothe in 1990. At the end of the decade, a nail bomb attack at the Admiral Duncan—a gay pub in London—killed three and injured seventy-nine. One result of the bombing was that the London police started to work with an independent LGBTQ+ advisory group.

A DEMONSTRATION THE DAY AFTER THE BOMBING OF THE ADMIRAL DUNCAN PUB

A CANDLELIT VIGIL FOR MATTHEW SHEPARD

Brandon Teena, a young American transgender man, was brutally raped and murdered in 1993 by former friends after they discovered his biological sex. Teena's tragic story was retold in the acclaimed film *Boys Don't Cry* (1999), drawing much-needed attention to how trans people are particularly vulnerable to hate crime.

However, it was the horrific murder of American student Matthew Shepard (see page 92) that truly woke the world up to the reality of homophobic hate crime. If any good could come out of such a senseless and barbaric act, it was the realization that society could no longer silently tolerate such bigotry and hatred.

HATE CRIME

Sadly, many LGBTQ+ people have been subjected to verbal abuse, bullying, intimidation, abusive messages, and physical attacks because of their perceived "difference." Hate incidents and crimes often go unreported, so it can be difficult to fully understand the extent of the problem. However, extreme acts of violence have raised awareness, such as the 2016 attack on the Pulse nightclub in Orlando, Florida, in which forty-nine people were murdered. The incidence of homophobic hate crime has risen sharply in recent years, and transgender people as well as Black, Asian, and minority ethnic LGBTQ+ people are particularly vulnerable.

> **" HOMOSEXUALITY IS PART OF SOCIETY**
> **I GUESS THAT THEY NEED MORE VARIETY**
> **FREEDOM OF EXPRESSION IS REALLY THE THING. "**
>
> FROM "AIN'T NOBODY STRAIGHT IN LA" (1975)
> BY THE MOTOWN GROUP THE MIRACLES

Following the Stonewall Riots in 1969 (see page 60), many LGBTQ+ movers and shakers shaped popular culture. While some remained closeted, other brave trailblazers chose to come out or were hiding in plain sight.

In 1970, legendary British singer Dusty Springfield courageously announced her bisexuality in a magazine interview. Two years later, David Bowie told a music journalist he was gay. Although he later said he had in fact been a "closet heterosexual," his gender-bending performances sent a message that "gayness" was something cool rather than shameful.

IN 2006, BOY GEORGE ANNOUNCED ON CAMERA THAT HE WAS "MILITANTLY GAY."

Although both Springfield and Bowie saw their music sales affected, they projected an "otherness" that countless LGBTQ+ people could relate to, and they paved the way for other LGBTQ+ artists to come out, such as Elton John in 1976. Meanwhile, Queen's flamboyant lead singer, Freddie Mercury, was never afraid to flaunt his sexuality, but neither did he ever align himself with the LGBTQ+ movement. For Mercury, who died of AIDS in 1991, his attitude to his sexuality seems to have been, "So what?"—and many would say that is a statement in itself.

As the AIDS crisis hit hard in the 1980s, LGBTQ+ artists became more cautious about explicitly stating their sexual identity. The gender-fluid frontman of Culture Club, Boy George, gave various answers when asked if he was gay. George Michael—of the 1980s pop duo Wham! and later a solo star—promoted a heterosexual image until he was publicly

outed in 1998. However, some, like Jimmy Sommerville of Bronski Beat, were out, loud and proud. His group's 1984 hit, "Smalltown Boy," spoke of the anguish that young LGBTQ+ people often face.

By the 1990s, homophobia was still widespread, but more and more people in the public eye were choosing to come out. Pop icon Madonna opened up LGBTQ+ culture to the mainstream with her videos showing gay dancers and same-sex kissing. Meanwhile, Canadian country star kd lang came out as a lesbian in 1992, increasing visibility for lesbian women. In 1998, the triumph of Israeli singer Dana International at the Eurovision Song Contest was a landmark moment for the visibility of the transgender community.

DANA PAVED THE WAY FOR OTHER LGBTQ+ EUROVISION PERFORMERS SUCH AS CONCHITA WURST.

ON-SCREEN LANDMARKS

In the decades following the Stonewall Riots, the lives of LGBTQ+ people became increasingly more visible in film and TV. Game-changing moments included the first positive portrayal of a gay male relationship in the 1972 TV film *That Certain Summer*; the first sympathetic portrayal of a transgender character in the American TV series *The Jeffersons* in 1975; the first lesbian kiss on British TV in the drama *Girl* in 1975; the box-office success of *La Cage aux Folles* in 1978, a French-Italian film about a gay couple; and the first gay male kiss on the British TV soap opera *Eastenders* in 1987. In 1993, the mainstream Hollywood film *Philadelphia* did much to change the conversation around AIDS, while in 1997, a staggering 42 million Americans tuned in to watch Ellen DeGeneres's title character come out in the sitcom *Ellen*.

MATTHEW SHEPARD

1976–1998

In 1998, the brutal torture and murder of Matthew Shepard, a gay twenty-one-year-old student, was a wake-up call for America and the world beyond. His parents, Dennis and Judy Shepard, were determined that something positive should come out of their son's terrible death—and it did. Thanks to their efforts, many LGBTQ+ people were galvanized into joining the movement against hate crime, and lawmakers were stung into tackling it.

On the face of it, there had been progress in 1990s America. The AIDS crisis had made the LGBTQ+ community a lot more visible, and it was now part of the cultural landscape. In the weeks before Shepard's death, *Will & Grace*, a TV sitcom featuring gay characters, had aired for the first time, and it would become a hugely influential hit. However, despite such gains, Matthew's murder showed that deep-rooted homophobia was still very much alive and well in society.

Openly gay, Matthew was a well-liked student at the University of Wyoming in the small town of Laramie. Studying languages, foreign relations, and political science, he dreamed of becoming a diplomat. On the day of his death, he had attended an LGBTQ+ student group meeting before going on to a bar. Sometime that evening, he fell into conversation with two young men, Aaron McKinney and Russell Henderson, and he left the bar with them.

The following day, a cyclist noticed what he thought at first was a scarecrow tied to a fence in a remote area. It was in fact Matthew. He had been severely

> **HATRED IS NOT NATURE. IT IS NURTURE. NO ONE IS BORN WITH HATRED IN THEIR HEART—IT IS LEARNED BEHAVIOR. PEOPLE LEARN TO HATE IN THE SAME WAY THEY LEARN TO LOVE. THE DIFFERENCE IS: WHO ARE THE EDUCATORS?**
>
> JUDY SHEPARD

beaten with the butt of a pistol, and left to die in near-freezing conditions. Still alive but unconscious, Matthew was rushed to hospital, but he died a few days later.

Matthew's gruesome death sent shock waves across America. In the following days, candlelight vigils were held around the country, including one attended by thousands outside the US Capitol Building. But there was an ugly side, too. Outside the church at Matthew's funeral, protesters held signs spewing antigay hatred.

The repercussions of Matthew's death were far-reaching. It has been the subject of books, films, and an acclaimed play, *The Laramie Project*, which has been performed worldwide. His family set up the Matthew Shepard Foundation with the mission to "erase hate by replacing it with understanding, compassion and acceptance." The foundation helped to expand federal hate crime law to include crimes motivated by gender, disability, or sexual orientation. In 2009, Judy and Dennis Shepard were at the White House to see it signed into law by the then-president, Barack Obama.

Judy and Dennis have traveled extensively, advocating for LGBTQ+ rights. In 2018, twenty years after Matthew's death, they watched his ashes being interred in Washington National Cathedral. Gene Robinson, an openly gay bishop, presided over the ceremony. Speaking of Dennis and Judy, he told the two thousand mourners, "By the grace of God, they decided they were going to turn this horrendous event into something good."

FLOWERS ON THE SPOT WHERE MATTHEW WAS TIED AFTER HIS SAVAGE ASSAULT

TOWARD EQUALITY

The road toward marriage equality has been a long and difficult one. Opponents argue that marriage is a union between a man and a woman. Some of those with religious or moral objections to same-sex relationships argue that granting equal rights to same-sex couples turns a "moral wrong" into a civil right or represents a danger to the traditional family structure.

Not all LGBTQ+ people agree that equal marriage is an important right, either. Some believe that copying a heterosexual tradition reinforces the idea that straight relationships are the norm. Some lesbians oppose marriage on feminist grounds because it has traditionally benefited men. But for many LGBTQ+ people, marriage is an important civil right: A lack of equality in the eyes of the law sends the message that LGBTQ+ lives matter less and that their relationships are less valid. In short, it's discrimination.

The fight for legal recognition for same-sex marriage may seem like a twenty-first-century battle, but the first small steps toward marriage equality were taken much earlier. In the years following the Stonewall Riots (see page 60), many same-sex couples applied for marriage licenses, though it was not until the 1990s that the push for equal marriage rights began to gather pace.

As small gains were made, opponents panicked and there was a backlash. In 1996, American president Bill Clinton signed the Defense of Marriage Act (DOMA), which defined marriage as the union between one man and one woman. This effectively denied same-sex couples the federal benefits, such as inheritance rights, that married heterosexual couples enjoyed. The act remained in place until 2013.

LICENSE TO MARRY

In 1970, law student Jack Baker and his partner Michael McConnell applied for a marriage license in Hennepin County, Minnesota, in the US. The application was refused, but Baker spotted a legal loophole. Jack changed his name to the gender-neutral "Pat Lyn," and the couple made another application in a different county. A clerk, not realizing that Pat Lyn was a man, issued a license. The couple were wed, and although the marriage was never officially recorded, neither was it dissolved. In 2018, a Minnesota judge ruled that the marriage was valid.

MICHAEL MCCONNELL (LEFT) AND JACK BAKER

In 2001, the Netherlands became the first country in the world to make it possible for same-sex couples to marry. The legislation also gave them the right to adopt children. Four same-sex couples were married in Amsterdam on the day the law came into effect.

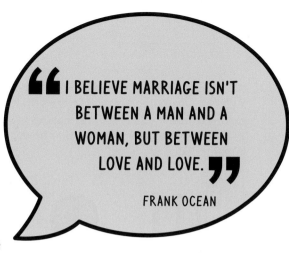

> **I BELIEVE MARRIAGE ISN'T BETWEEN A MAN AND A WOMAN, BUT BETWEEN LOVE AND LOVE.**
>
> FRANK OCEAN

Over the next few years, other countries followed suit, including Belgium (2003), Canada (2005), Spain (2005), and South Africa (2006). As of 2019, twenty-nine countries have made same-sex marriage legal.

In Britain, civil partnerships were introduced in 2004, giving same-sex couples the same rights as married couples but not the label of "marriage." Equal marriage was introduced in 2014, though not in Northern Ireland. Meanwhile, the Republic of Ireland became the first country in 2015 to legalize same-sex marriage after a popular vote.

In the US in 2000, Vermont was the first state to make civil partnerships legal, while in 2004, Massachusetts became the first to allow same-sex marriage. By the start of 2015, same-sex marriage was still illegal in thirteen states, but in June of that year, it was finally legalized across the nation.

In 2013, New Zealand became the first country in the Asia-Pacific region to allow same-sex marriage, while Australia decisively voted for it in 2017. For Penny Wong, Australia's first openly gay senator, the result was both a political victory and a moment of personal joy. In a moving speech, she said, "Equality never comes easy. . . . It was true of women fighting for suffrage. . . . It is true of Australia's first peoples, who have fought to be truly recognized as citizens of our nation, and it has been true for lesbian, gay, bisexual, transgender and intersex Australians fighting for equality before the law."

PENNY WONG SHED TEARS OF JOY WHEN THE RESULT OF THE VOTE WAS REVEALED.

Traditionally, society has understood a family to mean one man, one woman, and their children—and whether married or not, same-sex couples have often struggled to build a family life. As marriage equality has gradually become a reality in parts of the world, many legal barriers have fallen away. Most European countries now allow same-sex couples to adopt children, and this right was granted in the US in 2017 and in Australia in 2018. However, despite changes to the law, LGBTQ+ families still encounter prejudice and discrimination in their everyday lives.

TRANSGENDER PREGNANCY

In 2008, Thomas Beatie and his partner, Nancy, went public with the news that he was pregnant. Thomas had transitioned in his twenties, but had kept his female reproductive organs, so he was able to fall pregnant with the help of a sperm donor. The couple experienced many difficulties, such as the media poking fun at them, medical workers refusing to call Thomas "he," and a lack of support from family members. Thomas's story drew attention to gender identity and transgender issues, and showed how trans people often face an uphill struggle to find acceptance, even from within the LGBTQ+ community.

THOMAS BEATIE WITH HIS FIRST WIFE, NANCY. HE HAS BEEN PREGNANT THREE TIMES.

Given the long fight for LGBTQ+ rights, it's not surprising that the world has struggled to accept the idea of an LGBTQ+ person holding political power. However, the last two decades have seen a number of firsts.

In 2009, Iceland's Jóhanna Sigurðardóttir made history when she became the first openly LGBTQ+ person to become a country's prime minister. Elio Di Rupo became prime minister of Belgium in 2011, and Xavier Bettel was elected Luxembourg's prime minister in 2013. In Serbia, Ana Brnabić was elected leader in 2017, while Leo Varadkar became Ireland's prime minister in the same year.

The road to LGBTQ+ people participating in public life has been a long one with many pioneers along the way. In 1974, lesbian Kathy Kozachenko was the first openly LGBTQ+ person to successfully run for public office in the US, while Coos Huijsen of the Netherlands was the world's first openly gay person to become a member of parliament (MP) in 1976.

Others bravely followed: Italy's first openly gay MP was Angelo Pezzana in 1979. In Britain, Chris Smith became the country's first MP to voluntarily come out in 1984, while Waheed Ali was the first openly gay man to enter the House of Lords. In 1988, Canada's first openly gay MP was Svend Robinson, while Bob Brown became Australia's first out MP in 1996. In 2019, Taiga Ishikawa became the first openly gay person to be elected to Japan's national parliament.

TAIGA ISHIKAWA

Transgender politicians have been described as the "Cinderellas" of the LGBTQ+ community because of their struggle for visibility. In 1991, Joanne Marie Conte became the first trans woman to be elected to an American city council, while New Zealand's Georgina Beyer became the world's first openly trans mayor in 1995. In 2017, Tamara Adrián was the first trans person to be elected to political office in Venezuela. She has said that officials like her "are creating hope for those who have been excluded."

HAVE YOU HEARD OF?

Lou Sullivan (1951–1991)
This transgender activist and author was a pioneer of the female-to-male trans movement, and lobbied for the recognition of gay trans men.

Lisa Power (born 1954)
A longstanding LGBTQ+ rights campaigner who cofounded Stonewall UK and was the first openly gay or lesbian person to address the United Nations.

Jackie Kay (born 1961)
The Black Scottish poet, novelist, and Scottish Poet Laureate since 2016 has explored themes of sexuality and identity in her work.

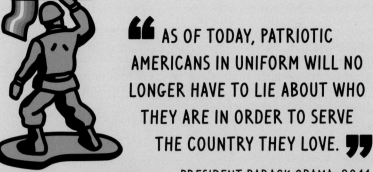

> **AS OF TODAY, PATRIOTIC AMERICANS IN UNIFORM WILL NO LONGER HAVE TO LIE ABOUT WHO THEY ARE IN ORDER TO SERVE THE COUNTRY THEY LOVE.**
>
> PRESIDENT BARACK OBAMA, 2011

FIGHTING PROUD

Over the decades, many LGBTQ+ men and women have been barred from serving in their country's military or have been rooted out and dismissed in disgrace. In 1993, the US introduced a "don't ask, don't tell" policy. Military personnel could not be asked about their sexual orientation, but neither could they be openly gay. This law was repealed in 2011, but a backward step was taken in 2017 when President Trump announced the military would no longer accept transgender individuals. In Britain, LGBTQ+ people have been allowed to serve openly in the armed forces since 2000. This is now the case in most western countries, as well as in Chile, Brazil, South Africa, and Israel.

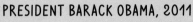

PROTESTS WERE HELD AGAINST TRUMP'S 2017 ANNOUNCEMENT.

Coming out can be enormously challenging in the world of sport. Society has fixed ideas about what an elite athlete should be, and being LGBTQ+ often flies in the face of what "maleness" or "strength" are thought to look like.

In the 1970s, American baseball player Glenn Burke was one of the first athletes to kick back against the status quo. Although he never publicly came out, he didn't hide his gay identity either. When the team management offered him $75,000 to get married, he refused. He retired at the age of twenty-seven, and tragically died of AIDS in 1995.

> **❝I'M A 34-YEAR-OLD NBA CENTER. I'M BLACK. AND I'M GAY. ❞**
>
> BASKETBALL STAR JASON COLLINS CAME OUT MID-CAREER IN 2013

In 1981, American tennis champion Billie Jean King hit the headlines when she was outed as a lesbian. Things became very difficult for her: She lost all her endorsements—worth $2 million—within twenty-four hours, and she was shamed and ridiculed by the media. King has since become a passionate activist for social equality.

BASEBALL'S FIRST OUT PLAYER, GLENN BURKE, IS CREDITED WITH INVENTING THE HIGH FIVE.

In the macho world of rugby league, Australian Ian Roberts was the first player—and high-profile Australian athletes—to come out, in 1995. He braved public abuse, but was also hailed as an inspiring role model. Meanwhile, Welsh rugby union star Gareth Thomas says he lifted the lid on "years of despair" when he came out as gay in 2009. Another stigma was challenged in 2019 when he revealed he was HIV positive.

The first openly transgender athlete to compete professionally was tennis player Renée Richards. When she was barred from the US Open, Richards filed a lawsuit, was declared legally female, and then competed in the 1977 event. Today, the issue of trans people competing in sport remains controversial, and trans athletes continue fighting for acceptance.

While homophobia remains in sport, the list of stars who have come out grows ever-longer. Among their number are Canadian Olympic ice hockey player Sarah Vaillancourt, transgender Thai boxing star Parinya Charoenphol, American ice skater Adam Rippon, Belgian tennis players Alison van Uytvanck and Greet Minnen (partners on and off court), British boxer Nicola Adams, American golfer Tadd Fujikawa, and Israeli Paralympic basketball player Moran Samuel.

NICOLA ADAMS, WHO IS BISEXUAL, WAS THE FIRST WOMAN TO WIN AN OLYMPIC BOXING TITLE.

JUSTIN FASHANU (1961–1998)

In 1990, Justin Fashanu—the first Black soccer player in Britain to be traded for more than a million pounds—took a huge professional and personal risk when he became the first top-level soccer player to come out as gay. As a Black man in 1980s Britain, Fashanu had already encountered racism. Now, as a gay soccer player, he faced a vicious backlash from fans and a lack of support from his club and family. He ended his life in 1998 at the age of thirty-seven. Soccer has been described as the "last bastion" of homophobia in sport—in the two decades since Fashanu's death, there have been no openly LGBTQ+ soccer players in the top tiers of the men's game.

THE PRESENTERS OF *QUEER EYE*

With the push toward inclusion, the twenty-first century has seen the lives of LGBTQ+ characters increasingly represented in TV and film—and more and more celebrities are proudly embracing their sexual identities and actively fighting for LGBTQ+ rights.

Mainstream TV shows like *Orange Is the New Black* (2013–2019), *Queer Eye* (2018–), and *Pose* (2018–), and films such as *Brokeback Mountain* (2005), *Carol* (2015), and *A Fantastic Woman* (2017) have a direct impact on how we view our world. That's why it's so important that they show a diverse range of characters and feature stories that accurately reflect the society we live in. For young LGBTQ+ people particularly, who might be struggling to embrace their sexual identity, it's incredibly important to see people and stories in the media that they identify with. For example, *How Gay is Pakistan?*, a 2015 documentary made by Pakistani-British comic Mawaan Rizwan, explores why coming out to his parents was so difficult.

It's no longer the case that identifying as LGBTQ+ is a career-ending moment, but in this modern age of social media, stars are more vulnerable than ever to homophobic abuse and personal attacks. But out-and-proud celebrities—such as English musician and LGBTQ+ activist Olly Alexander, outspoken actor Elliot Page, and model Cara Delevingne, who brought bisexuality to the mainstream—play important roles in fighting discrimination and helping the LGBTQ+ community feel more connected and less isolated.

CARA DELEVINGNE

> **" IF YOU'RE A 12-YEAR-OLD AND BEGINNING TO WONDER ABOUT YOURSELF, THEN SEEING [LGBTQ+] PEOPLE IN PUBLIC TALKING ABOUT THE LIFE THEY'RE LIVING IS SO IMPORTANT. "**
>
> RUSSELL T. DAVIES, CREATOR OF TV WORKS SUCH AS *QUEER AS FOLK* AND *DOCTOR WHO*

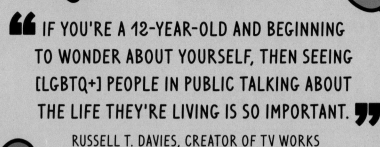

LAVERNE COX (BORN 1972)

Laverne Cox shot to fame when she played the role of prisoner Sophia Burset in the Netflix show *Orange Is the New Black*. As the first openly transgender woman of color to be nominated for a Primetime Emmy Award in an acting role, Laverne became a history-maker. In 2014, she again broke new ground when she was featured on the cover of *Time* magazine with the title "The Transgender Tipping Point." Laverne told the magazine's readers how she was bullied as a child and of her struggles to find acceptance. Her interview helped to educate people about how trans people are so often marginalized and misunderstood.

CHRISTINE AND THE QUEENS

BORN 1988

Global pop star Christine and the Queens —also known as Chris—is as famous for her shape-shifting and playing with gender ideas as she is for singing and dancing. As someone attracted to people regardless of their sex or gender identity, she has brought pansexuality into the mainstream.

Christine was born Héloïse Létissier in Nantes, France. As a child, she loved music and dance, and by the age of four was taking ballet and piano lessons. Létissier realized she was "queer" at a very young age, but although she felt some inner shame, she says her parents never made a big deal about her sexuality.

In 2008, she began studying drama in Lyon and then in Paris. She wanted to be a theater director, but when she found out that only the boys in her course had permission to direct, she staged her own play—and ended up being expelled. Around the same time, she suffered a traumatic relationship breakup with her girlfriend. Feeling angry and depressed, Létissier withdrew and began writing plays, creating an outlet for her fury in the form of a character called "Christine."

In 2010, on a trip to London, Létissier watched three drag queens perform in a gay club. They took her under their wing and helped her to realize that it was okay to bend the rules—and that she would feel empowered by embracing who she really was.

This was the point that Christine and the Queens was truly born—a solo act that references the importance of her drag-queen friends. She had two tattoos emblazoned on her forearms—"We accept you" and "One of us."

Christine's debut album was *Chaleur Humaine (Human Warmth)*, first released in France in 2014. Many of the tracks explore ideas around gender and sexuality. In the first track, "iT," Christine declares, "I'm a man now." The album sold 1 million copies worldwide and, by 2017, had been streamed 194 million times.

In interviews, Christine is frank about how she is "gender-fluid." Rather than play it safe, for her second album, she decided to cut her hair short and start again as "Chris." The album's second song, "Girlfriend," was ranked song of the year in 2018 by *Time* magazine.

In April 2019, Christine and the Queens performed a rendition of RuPaul's iconic hit "Sissy That Walk" on the season 11 finale of *RuPaul's Drag Race*. Perhaps the song's lyrics were fitting for Christine—or Chris: "And if I fly, or if I fall / Least I can say, I gave it all."

Christine has not been afraid to push the boundaries or speak her truth. She has often faced criticism and even mockery, especially in her native France. But as she said after coming out as pansexual in 2014, "Embracing my queerness sparks my life as an artist."

"THERE'S JUST ONE RULE FOR THIS GIG. YOU GET TO BE WHOEVER YOU WANT TO BE. THERE IS NO JUDGEMENT HERE, ONLY LOVE."

CHRISTINE AND THE QUEENS PERFORMING AT LATITUDE FESTIVAL IN ENGLAND, JULY 2016

CULTURE MILESTONES

Today, LGBTQ+ artists are largely part of mainstream culture, but moving out of the shadows has been a long, uphill struggle. Along the way, there have been many trailblazers and breakthrough moments—the following are just a few of the highlights.

THE FIRST GAY NOVELS

The first American gay novel is widely considered to be Bayard Taylor's *Joseph and His Friend: A Story of Pennsylvania*, published in 1870. In 1906, *Imre: A Memorandum* by Edward Prime-Stevenson was greatly influential because of its positive portrayal of a homosexual relationship.

VIRGINIA WOOLF'S *ORLANDO*

Woolf's landmark 1928 novel romps through four hundred years of history, playfully exploring gender fluidity. Orlando is an Elizabethan nobleman who halfway through the story wakes up as a woman—and travels on in this new female form toward the twentieth century. Woolf's cross-dressing lover, Vita Sackville-West, provided the inspiration for the novel.

> **"** DIFFERENT THOUGH THE SEXES ARE, THEY INTER-MIX. IN EVERY HUMAN BEING, A VACILLATION FROM ONE SEX TO THE OTHER TAKES PLACE, AND OFTEN IT IS ONLY THE CLOTHES THAT KEEP THE MALE OR FEMALE LIKENESS, WHILE UNDERNEATH THE SEX IS THE VERY OPPOSITE OF WHAT IT IS ABOVE. **"**

VIRGINA WOOLF,
ORLANDO, 1928

THE COLOR PURPLE

Alice Walker's extraordinary 1982 novel won the Pulitzer Prize and was later turned into a successful movie. In *The Color Purple*, Celie, a Black girl growing up in 1930s rural America, suffers poverty and violent abuse, but ultimately finds love, healing, and happiness with a woman.

GLORIA GAYNOR

OVER THE RAINBOW

Empowering "gay anthems" carry messages of hope, defiance, and above all, pride. One of the first songs to make its mark was Judy Garland's "Over the Rainbow," recorded in 1939. The most famous gay anthem is arguably Gloria Gaynor's 1978 disco hit "I Will Survive."

THE FIRST OPENLY GAY ROCK SINGER

In the early 1970s, Bruce Wayne Campbell—or "Jobriath"—hit the glam-rock scene in a blaze of publicity. He was billed as the "new Bowie," but the American public wasn't ready for his flamboyant, unashamed homosexuality, and the expected superstardom never arrived. He died aged thirty-six from AIDS in 1983.

FILM FIRSTS

Released in 1919, *Different from the Others* was a groundbreaking film by Magnus Hirschfeld about a love affair between two male musicians. Another German film, *Girls in Uniform*, released in 1931, was one of the first films to explore lesbian love. In 1985 the British film *My Beautiful Laundrette* tackled complex interracial British and Pakistani gay relationships.

GIRLS IN UNIFORM

A FANTASTIC WOMAN

Transgender representation in cinema experienced a watershed moment in 2018. Trans lives had been depicted before in mainstream films like *Boys Don't Cry* (1999) and *The Danish Girl* (2015), but the transgender roles were played by cisgender actors. In the Chilean film *A Fantastic Woman*, which won the Academy Award for best foreign language film, the trans protagonist is played by trans actor Daniela Vega.

WHY I HAVE PRIDE

Name

EZRA LEE

Age

21

Identifies as

TRANSGENDER MALE

Pride is authentic and unapologetic; it's how we celebrate the diversity of the LGBTQ+ community. It allows us to memorialize the incomprehensible struggle we have gone through to get to where we are today and to remind everybody that we still have a long way to go.

Pride, to me, means feeling happy with my identity, and exuding that feeling wherever I go and whatever I do. During my adolescence, the process of grasping my identity was terrifying and exhausting. I explored my identity and sexuality, and this, combined with severe mental health problems, was a tedious procedure. Although I'm very lucky to have had a somewhat okay experience when I came out to friends and family, it took me many years to be at peace with myself, to be patient, and to reach a point of tranquility. Personal growth becomes really addictive once you realize that it's always possible to improve your experience of being.

Society simultaneously shines a spotlight on the transgender individuals who pass, and ridicules and doubts the ones who don't. I've found that cisgender people tend to be strangely magnetized by the physical transformation of transgender lives. Transgender individuals are often fetishized with no repercussions. But the invisibility and poverty that transgender people often suffer, and the horrifyingly high rate of violent hate crime directed at them, is not cute or glamorous. Having been on hormone therapy for over a year, I'm now reaching the point where I pass in public. I often hope that when people pass me by, they unconsciously think to themselves, "That's a man." Having that public sense of validation is important, as it brings me an insane amount of euphoria.

> **IT'S OKAY TO NOT KNOW WHAT YOUR SEXUAL PREFERENCE OR GENDER IDENTITY IS. YOU DON'T HAVE TO LABEL IT TO FEEL VALID.**

This past year has been a journey of self-expression, not just physically but spiritually, too. I've surrounded myself with people that reflect who I want to be and how I want to feel, which has massively benefited me mentally and emotionally. I grew tired of trying to fit into a specific narrative. I used to wake up every day with no motivation to exist, constantly thinking, "What's the point?" But now I'm excited to grow and flourish as an individual and hopefully make an impact as a queer transgender creative. It's a constant and often scary process— but I'm taking every day as it comes, and that's okay.

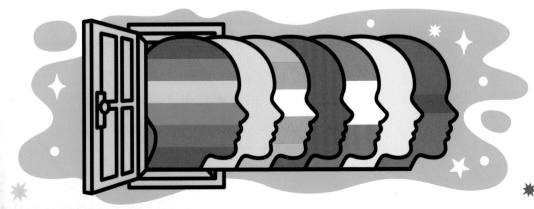

THE
FIGHT
GOES ON

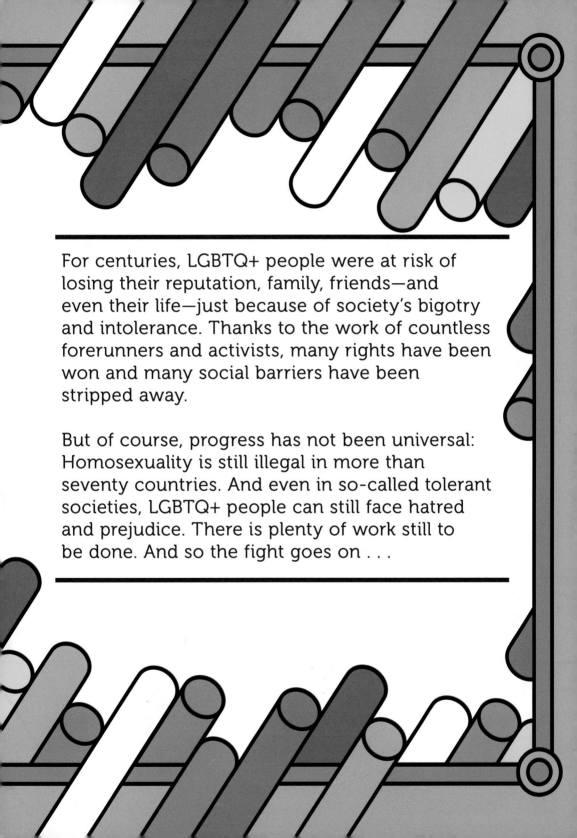

For centuries, LGBTQ+ people were at risk of losing their reputation, family, friends—and even their life—just because of society's bigotry and intolerance. Thanks to the work of countless forerunners and activists, many rights have been won and many social barriers have been stripped away.

But of course, progress has not been universal: Homosexuality is still illegal in more than seventy countries. And even in so-called tolerant societies, LGBTQ+ people can still face hatred and prejudice. There is plenty of work still to be done. And so the fight goes on . . .

THE LGBTQ+ COMMUNITY TODAY

In June 2019, jubilant LGBTQ+ rights campaigners in Africa celebrated a major victory when Botswana decriminalized homosexuality. One of the judges stated, "Human dignity is harmed when minority groups are marginalized."

LGBTQ+ rights have come a long way in the past few decades, but the fight isn't over. Around the world, people face violence, torture, and even death simply for who they love and who they are. In much of Africa, the Middle East, Asia, and parts of the Americas, homosexuality is still illegal.

Homosexuality is legal in all European countries, but rights and protections vary widely. In Russia, for example, it's dangerous to be visibly out. In 2013, a "gay propaganda" law was introduced. It bans the promotion of homosexuality, which has had the effect of preventing young people from accessing information about LGBTQ+ issues. Since the law was passed, homophobic attacks have rocketed.

Although LGBTQ+ people everywhere are vulnerable to discrimination and hate crime, the situation for transgender people is particularly challenging. Around the world, they frequently encounter hatred and violence. They must also battle legal obstacles in order to have their gender recognized, to access services, and to enjoy equal opportunities. Organizations such as Canadian charity Rainbow Railroad do vital work in helping LGBTQ+ people living in fear to escape to a safer country.

WE ARE MADE FOR GOODNESS. WE ARE MADE FOR LOVE. . . . WE ARE MADE TO TELL THE WORLD THAT THERE ARE NO OUTSIDERS. ALL ARE WELCOME: BLACK, WHITE, RED, YELLOW, RICH, POOR, EDUCATED, NOT EDUCATED, MALE, FEMALE, GAY, STRAIGHT, ALL, ALL, ALL. 🙶🙶

ARCHBISHOP DESMOND TUTU, NOBEL PEACE PRIZE WINNER

ACTIVISTS CELEBRATE THE DECRIMINALIZATION OF HOMOSEXUALITY IN BOTSWANA IN 2019.

COLONIAL LAWS

Even though Britain's own laws against homosexuality were revoked more than fifty years ago, versions of the same laws live on in many countries that were once part of the British Empire. In fact, more than thirty countries that were once British colonies—such as Pakistan, Malaysia, and Kenya—still have the same harsh anti-LGBTQ+ legislation that was put in place during colonial rule. In 2018, the then prime minister, Theresa May, apologized for Britain's colonial legacy: "I am all too aware that these laws were put in place by my country. They were wrong then and they are wrong now."

In the past, being LGBTQ+ could be incredibly scary and lonely—and of course, that is still the case for people in many parts of the world. But LGBTQ+ people have always found ways to find and connect with each other, and since the Stonewall Riots, countless community groups have thrived.

Today, many gay bars, nightclubs, and other dedicated spaces offer LGBTQ+ people the chance to get together in a "safe," nonjudgmental environment. These spaces tend to be concentrated in urban areas, so LGBTQ+ people living in more rural areas can still feel excluded, as well as older people and those with financial restrictions or disabilities. As the deadly 2016 Pulse nightclub attack in Orlando, Florida, showed, homophobia can still rear its ugly head. Nevertheless, it's vitally important that there are places where LGBTQ+ people can feel free to be themselves.

Online spaces and communities also provide important ways for LGBTQ+ people to connect with each other and to explore and make sense of their identity. Of course, LGBTQ+ people can experience hate and harassment online, but the internet can also be a place of refuge for those looking to express who they are.

THE GAY'S THE WORD BOOKSHOP IN LONDON IS A THRIVING COMMUNITY SPACE.

HAVE YOU HEARD OF?

Claire Harvey (born 1974)
The only openly lesbian athlete at the London 2012 Paralympics, Harvey is a champion of diversity and inclusion in sports and education.

Pete Buttigieg (born 1982)
This American politician became the first openly gay candidate for president when he launched his bid for the Democratic nomination in April 2019.

Nikkie de Jager (born 1994)
Better known as NikkieTutorials, this Dutch beauty influencer, with over 13 million YouTube subscribers, made headlines when she revealed her trans identity in 2020.

Today, there's growing awareness that the concept of a single LGBTQ+ community is not always helpful. In the long fight for equality, LGBTQ+ people have often found strength in numbers, but it's also important to remember that within the community, there exist people with vastly different experiences and needs. For example, trans people; Black, Indigenous, and people of color (BIPOC); people of faith; and disabled people may all experience real feelings of exclusion, even within the LGBTQ+ community.

SCHOOLS OUT

Many young LGBTQ+ people experience bullying due to their sexual orientation—this can lead to missed school, underachievement, and poor mental health. It's really important that schools are safe spaces for both LGBTQ+ teachers and students. Teachers play a vital role in supporting young LGBTQ+ people, helping them to be proud of who they are and ensuring they are not disadvantaged in any way. Charities like Schools OUT UK and Just Like Us in Britain, and the Gay, Lesbian and Straight Education Network (GLSEN) in the US, do vital work to promote LGBTQ+ inclusion and awareness in schools.

MARIELLE FRANCO
1979–2018

In March 2018, Marielle Franco—
a Black, openly bisexual politician
—paid the ultimate price when she was
gunned down in Rio de Janeiro, Brazil.
She had fought courageously for LGBTQ+,
Black, and women's rights in Brazil, and her death has become
a symbol of social inequality. Her murder demonstrated
that powerful forces often try to shut down the voices of
vulnerable minority groups.

Franco was born into a family of migrants in a favela (slum) of Rio de Janeiro.
Brazil's slums are areas of great poverty, violence, and crime, and their residents
are regarded as socially inferior. Growing up in this kind of environment,
Franco understood very early on what it was to experience discrimination and
a lack of opportunity.

After having a daughter at the age of nineteen, Franco studied for a degree
in social sciences at university. Her interest in human rights had been ignited
when a friend was killed by a stray bullet in a shootout between police and drug
dealers. She joined the Party of Socialism and Liberty (PSOL), where she became
a rising star. In 2016, Franco ran for office as a candidate for Rio's city council.
Her election caused a stir. As a Black, bisexual, single mother born in a slum,
the outspoken politician was a minority many times over.

On the face of it, LGBTQ+ rights in Brazil look advanced: Same-sex marriage has
been legal since 2013, and São Paulo is home to the world's largest gay Pride.

Yet, a recent surge of far-right politics has accompanied a steep rise in homophobic hate crime. In fact, Brazil is reported to have the highest rate of LGBTQ+ murders in the world.

Franco met her partner, Mônica Benício, thirteen years before her death. The couple lived with Franco's daughter, and they were planning to marry. On the night of her murder, Franco was returning from a meeting about empowering Black women. Assailants opened fire on her car, killing both her and the driver.

Franco's death bore all the hallmarks of a politically motivated killing —and it sent a sinister message that those speaking up for human rights were not welcome in Brazil. Thousands gathered to protest in cities across Brazil, while Amnesty International and Human Rights Watch condemned the killing. Franco's death was a rallying cry to activists everywhere. Her name lives on, and the voices she represented have not been silenced. The struggle must go on.

"MARIELLE PRESENTE! (MARIELLE IS WITH US!)"

RALLYING CRY AT PROTESTS FOLLOWING FRANCO'S DEATH

WHY I HAVE PRIDE

Name

MOHAMMED BARBER

Age

24

Identifies as

GAY / QUEER

With this short article I am coming out to the world. Hello world, Queer Muslim here. This is the first time I've put my face next to an article about being gay. I've given interviews and written stuff before, but being named "Mohammed" is as good as being anonymous amongst Muslims. So this is a big milestone on what has been a long road.

Let's rewind back to the summer of 2013. I'd injured my foot, and all the sitting around finally forced me to confront the fact I like boys. It threw me into a spiral of depression and anxiety. Also, it was Ramadhan, which threw the whole gay Muslim contradiction into crescent-like clarity. Seeing I was in pain, Mum asked me what was wrong. I broke down in floods of tears and came out to her. She took it a lot better than I expected—I was shocked into relief. But this was just the first step. Dark days followed as I navigated the high seas of community, religion, family, friends, and the final year of university. It was not fun.

Much to my surprise, my Muslim friends took it a lot better than I expected. Acceptance from friends was one thing, but there was something I needed even more—acceptance within my religion. The turning point came when I spoke to a local imam. He told me sexuality cannot be changed, implying it was natural. I was stunned by his revelation. He'd basically told me that you cannot pray the gay away!

Then came some intense soul searching to deconstruct "truths" I was taught as a kid, and find a new narrative. I was up against the community that had raised me, and centuries of religious interpretation, all fused with the layers of self-hatred and insecurity that most LGBTQ+ people have.

>
> ## SELF-ACCEPTANCE IS A LONG-HAUL JOURNEY. YOU MUST FIND IT FOR YOURSELF AND TAKE OTHERS WITH YOU. WE NEED SUPPORT FROM EACH OTHER.

It took months, but I got there. I would not have made it if not for others. Finding your community is crucial. They will support and accept but also challenge you. It's not been easy. There are good days and bad days. I still don't have all my shit together, but I'm in a much better place to deal with it than before.

My friends, I leave you with words from an Indian trans activist that have proved endlessly inspirational to me: "Run to life."

LGBTQ+ MILESTONES

Many hurdles have been overcome in the fight for LGBTQ+ rights since the late nineteenth century. Decriminalizing homosexual acts is key, but it has meant different things in different countries, both in terms of enforcing the law and societal attitudes. Not all of the hurdles can be mentioned here, but these are some major highlights:

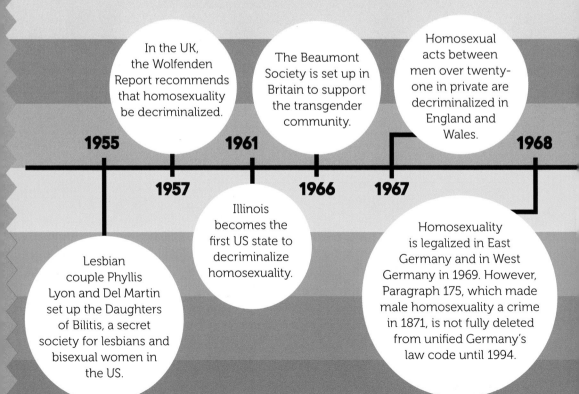

In the UK, the Wolfenden Report recommends that homosexuality be decriminalized.

The Beaumont Society is set up in Britain to support the transgender community.

Homosexual acts between men over twenty-one in private are decriminalized in England and Wales.

1955

1957

1961

1966

1967

1968

Illinois becomes the first US state to decriminalize homosexuality.

Lesbian couple Phyllis Lyon and Del Martin set up the Daughters of Bilitis, a secret society for lesbians and bisexual women in the US.

Homosexuality is legalized in East Germany and in West Germany in 1969. However, Paragraph 175, which made male homosexuality a crime in 1871, is not fully deleted from unified Germany's law code until 1994.

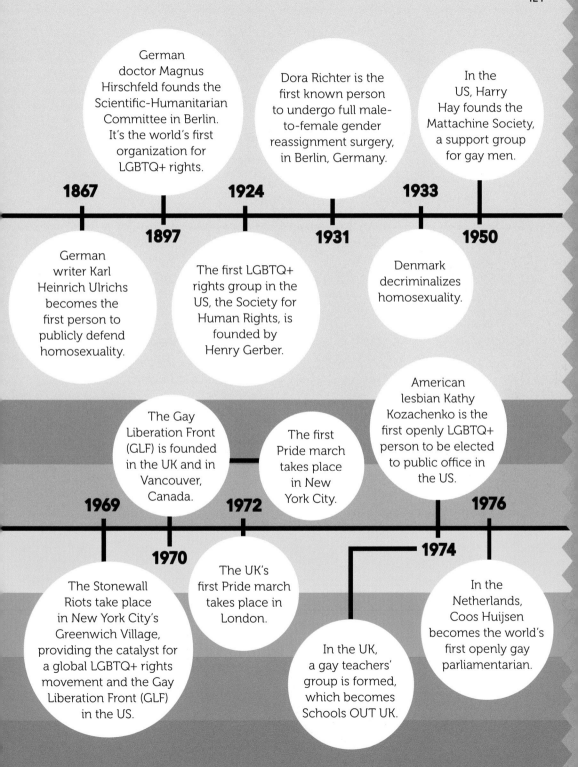

1867
German writer Karl Heinrich Ulrichs becomes the first person to publicly defend homosexuality.

German doctor Magnus Hirschfeld founds the Scientific-Humanitarian Committee in Berlin. It's the world's first organization for LGBTQ+ rights.

1897

1924
The first LGBTQ+ rights group in the US, the Society for Human Rights, is founded by Henry Gerber.

Dora Richter is the first known person to undergo full male-to-female gender reassignment surgery, in Berlin, Germany.

1931
Denmark decriminalizes homosexuality.

1933

In the US, Harry Hay founds the Mattachine Society, a support group for gay men.

1950

1969
The Stonewall Riots take place in New York City's Greenwich Village, providing the catalyst for a global LGBTQ+ rights movement and the Gay Liberation Front (GLF) in the US.

The Gay Liberation Front (GLF) is founded in the UK and in Vancouver, Canada.

1970
The UK's first Pride march takes place in London.

The first Pride march takes place in New York City.

1972

In the UK, a gay teachers' group is formed, which becomes Schools OUT UK.

1974

American lesbian Kathy Kozachenko is the first openly LGBTQ+ person to be elected to public office in the US.

1976
In the Netherlands, Coos Huijsen becomes the world's first openly gay parliamentarian.

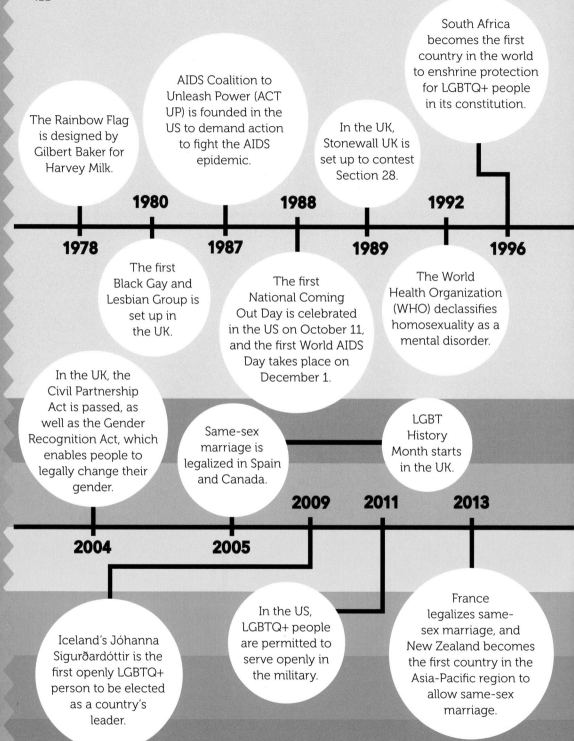

The Rainbow Flag is designed by Gilbert Baker for Harvey Milk.

AIDS Coalition to Unleash Power (ACT UP) is founded in the US to demand action to fight the AIDS epidemic.

In the UK, Stonewall UK is set up to contest Section 28.

South Africa becomes the first country in the world to enshrine protection for LGBTQ+ people in its constitution.

1980

1988

1992

1978

1987

1989

1996

The first Black Gay and Lesbian Group is set up in the UK.

The first National Coming Out Day is celebrated in the US on October 11, and the first World AIDS Day takes place on December 1.

The World Health Organization (WHO) declassifies homosexuality as a mental disorder.

In the UK, the Civil Partnership Act is passed, as well as the Gender Recognition Act, which enables people to legally change their gender.

Same-sex marriage is legalized in Spain and Canada.

LGBT History Month starts in the UK.

2009

2011

2013

2004

2005

Iceland's Jóhanna Sigurðardóttir is the first openly LGBTQ+ person to be elected as a country's leader.

In the US, LGBTQ+ people are permitted to serve openly in the military.

France legalizes same-sex marriage, and New Zealand becomes the first country in the Asia-Pacific region to allow same-sex marriage.

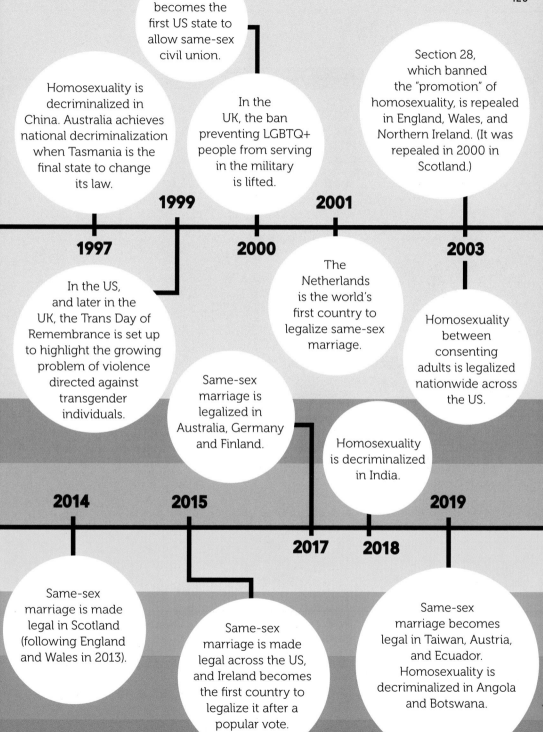

Vermont becomes the first US state to allow same-sex civil union.

Homosexuality is decriminalized in China. Australia achieves national decriminalization when Tasmania is the final state to change its law.

In the UK, the ban preventing LGBTQ+ people from serving in the military is lifted.

Section 28, which banned the "promotion" of homosexuality, is repealed in England, Wales, and Northern Ireland. (It was repealed in 2000 in Scotland.)

1999

1997

2000

2001

2003

In the US, and later in the UK, the Trans Day of Remembrance is set up to highlight the growing problem of violence directed against transgender individuals.

The Netherlands is the world's first country to legalize same-sex marriage.

Same-sex marriage is legalized in Australia, Germany and Finland.

Homosexuality between consenting adults is legalized nationwide across the US.

Homosexuality is decriminalized in India.

2014

2015

2017

2018

2019

Same-sex marriage is made legal in Scotland (following England and Wales in 2013).

Same-sex marriage is made legal across the US, and Ireland becomes the first country to legalize it after a popular vote.

Same-sex marriage becomes legal in Taiwan, Austria, and Ecuador. Homosexuality is decriminalized in Angola and Botswana.

GLOSSARY

ACTIVISM Taking a stand against an injustice

BIGOTRY Disliking those who hold different views or have a different way of life

BISEXUAL Describes a person who is attracted to people of more than one gender

BOHEMIAN Not following the rules of society, in an artistic way

BUGGERY A slang term for sodomy, or anal intercourse

CABARET Live entertainment of singing and dancing

CISGENDER Describes a person whose gender identity matches the sex they were assigned at birth

CIVIL PARTNERSHIP A legally recognized relationship between two people

CLOSET LGBTQ+ people who have not revealed their identity are described as "in the closet" or "closeted"

COLD WAR The tense conflict between the United States and the Soviet Union, 1946–1991

COLONIAL Relating to a country that rules other countries

CONCENTRATION CAMP A place where a large number of people are imprisoned in harsh conditions

CONFORMITY Going along with accepted beliefs and behavior

CROSS-DRESSING Wearing clothes associated with the opposite sex

DISCRIMINATION Treating someone as inferior, because of their race, gender, sexuality, or for other reasons

DRAG BALL An underground LGBTQ+ culture that thrived in the 1920s, where people, often drag queens, competed for glory and trophies

DRAG QUEEN A person, usually male, who dresses in women's clothing and turns it into a theatrical performance

DYKE A slang, often offensive, term for a lesbian

FANATICISM Extreme beliefs that can lead to unreasonable behavior

FASCISM A political system with a powerful leader and no room for opposing views

FEMINIST A person who tries to achieve equal opportunities for women

FEMME FATALE An attractive woman who brings trouble for those who fall for her charms

GAY Someone who is attracted to the same sex. It more commonly describes male relationships, but is frequently used to describe lesbian relationships, too

GENDER FLUID A gender identity that is not fixed, and can change over time

GENDER REASSIGNMENT SURGERY Surgery that changes a transgender person's body characteristics to match their gender identity

GENDER VARIANCE Describing the idea that there are many types of gender expression

GREAT DEPRESSION A worldwide economic crisis that lasted from 1929 to 1941

GROSS INDECENCY A term used in British law to describe certain criminal offenses, particularly sexual activity between men

HEMOPHILIAC Someone who has hemophilia, a condition that stops the blood from clotting properly

HETEROSEXUAL A person attracted to the opposite sex

HOMOPHOBIA The fear or dislike of LGBTQ+ people

HOMOSEXUAL A person who is attracted to someone of the same sex

INALIENABLE Something that can't be removed

INTERSEX Someone whose biological sex doesn't fit the terms of "male" or "female"

LAVENDER MARRIAGE A marriage intended to hide the sexual identity of one or both partners

LESBIAN A woman who is attracted to women

LGBTQ+ The acronym for lesbian, gay, bisexual, transgender, and queer or questioning. The "+" includes other identities

MANSLAUGHTER The unlawful killing of someone, where the killer didn't intend to do it or cannot be held responsible

NAZI Refers to Adolf Hitler's political party, the National Socialist German Workers' Party

NEO-NAZI Someone who is inspired by Hitler's political beliefs

NONBINARY Describes a gender identity that falls outside the terms of "male" or "female"

PANSEXUAL Someone who is attracted to other people, regardless of their biological sex or gender identity

PANSY CLUB Underground clubs with LGBTQ+ performers that thrived during the so-called "Pansy craze," in the 1920s and early 1930s

PENAL CODE A code of laws concerning crimes and punishments

PERSECUTION The ill-treatment of people because of their race, gender, sexuality, or other reasons

PREJUDICE An unfavorable opinion formed without knowledge or reason

PROPAGANDA Information, often misleading, intended to influence people

PROSTITUTE A person who engages in sexual activity for payment

QUAKER A faith group committed to peace

QUEER An intentionally vague term to describe someone who doesn't follow society's norms around sexuality or gender

SCHIZOPHRENIA A severe mental condition often involving delusions and disordered thinking

SEXUAL IDENTITY How you see and express yourself sexually

SPEAKEASY A bar selling illegal alcohol

STAR OF DAVID A symbol associated with the Jewish faith

STATUS QUO The existing state of affairs

STEREOTYPE A set idea that people hold about someone or something, which is often wrong

STRAIGHT Describes a person who is attracted to someone of the opposite sex

THEOLOGIAN Someone who studies God and religion

TRANSGENDER OR TRANS Describes a person who has a gender identity that differs from their sex assigned at birth

TURING'S LAW A law introduced in 2017 to pardon men convicted in the past because of their sexuality

UNDERGROUND A secret, often illegal, movement

VETO To refuse to allow something

WITCH HUNT An attempt to find and punish a particular group of people

INDEX

FURTHER INFORMATION

There are many online resources that offer advice and support for the issues facing young LGBTQ+ people.

The GLAAD Youth Engagement Program works to build a network of LGBTQ youth and allies across the nation who promote LGBTQ acceptance through the media.
www.glaad.org/youth

GLSEN works to end bullying and discrimination based on sexual orientation, gender identity, and/or gender expression. Additionally, they encourage LGBTQ cultural inclusion and awareness in K–12 schools.
www.glsen.org
(212) 727-0135

GSA Network creates student-run clubs that unite LGBTQ+ students and allies to build a safer and more supportive school community. Their clubs offer social interaction, support, and activism opportunities for their members.
www.gsanetwork.org
(415) 552-4229

The It Gets Better Project aims to connect young LGBTQ+ people with the global community. Among their resources are many uplifting videos showing young people sharing their stories of resilience and determination.
www.itgetsbetter.org

The LGBT National Help Center is a resource for lesbian, gay, bisexual, transgender, queer, and questioning youth. It provides a free and confidential hotline for peer support and finding local resources. The group also offers weekly youth chatrooms for young LGBTQ people to connect with supportive communities.
www.glbtnationalhelpcenter.org
LGBT National Youth Talkline:
(800) 246-7743

PFLAG is the first and largest organization for LGBTQ+ people, their parents and families, and allies.
www.pflag.org
(202) 467-8180

Q Chat Space provides online discussion groups for LGBTQ+ teens ages thirteen to nineteen that are facilitated by experienced staff who work at LGBTQ+ centers around the country.
www.qchatspace.org
954-765-6024

The Trevor Project focuses on suicide prevention efforts among lesbian, gay, bisexual, transgender, queer, and questioning youth. Available 24/7.
www.thetrevorproject.org
(866) 488-7386